STEM
THINKING SKILLS
in

Spatial Relation

and

Spatial Ability

by
MindMine

 Why this book?

Spatial ability is becoming increasingly important with the development of new technologies in Science, Technology, Engineering and Mathematics (STEM). Ability to understand organization of objects in space and applying spatial reasoning are key for success in solving many tasks in everyday life. "**STEM Thinking in Spatial Relation and Spatial Ability**" provides a solid foundation to fundamental skills and help to improve STEM thinking.

This book covers 3 areas and helps in:

Mechanical Reasoning:
Improve the ability to deduce relationships between mechanical parts

Spatial-Relational Thinking
Improve the ability to visualize 2-D figures and understand 3 dimensional spatial visualization

Abstract Reasoning
Improve the ability to find logical relationships in figure patterns

📚 What is covered?

This book extensively covers **FIGURE ANALOGIES** section of **Non-Verbal Battery** (Approximately 220 unique questions) and another 250 secondary questions.

📚 ONE FULL LENGTH PRACTICE TEST with Answers

Full Length Practice Test	20 Questions
📚 SPATIAL ABILITY - **MECHANICAL REASONING**	40 Questions
📚 Three-Dimensional **SPATIAL RELATIONAL THINKING**	35 Questions
📚 Two-dimensional **SPATIAL RELATIONAL THINKING**	30 Questions
📚 SPATIAL THINKING - **ABSTRACT REASONING**	30 Questions
📚 SPATIAL ABILITY - **RELATIONAL THINKING**	5 Questions

Table of Contents

Concept	Page#
Full Length Practice Test	1
SPATIAL ABILITY - MECHANICAL REASONING	16
Three-Dimensional SPATIAL RELATIONAL THINKING	47
Two-Dimensional SPATIAL RELATIONAL THINKING	96
SPATIAL THINKING - ABSTRACT REASONING	117
SPATIAL ABILITY - RELATIONAL THINKING	151
Answers	157

SPATIAL THINKING

FULL LENGTH TEST

1 — If gear **X** turns in clockwise direction, how does gear **C and D** turn?

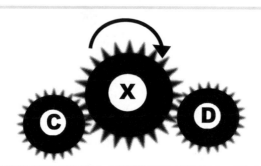

Both Clockwise, Slower than X	Both Counter Clockwise, Slower than X	C- Clockwise, D- Counter Clockwise Faster than X	D- Clockwise, C- Counter Clockwise Faster than X	Both Counter Clockwise, faster than X
1	2	3	4	5

2 — If **A** moves LEFT, how does gears turn?

Both Clockwise	Both Counter-Clockwise	1- Clockwise, 2- Counter Clockwise	2- Clockwise, 1- Counter Clockwise	Neither direction
1	2	3	4	5

3 — If bar **A** moves LEFT at a constant speed, how does bar B turn?

Right, Faster than A	Left, Faster than A	Right, Slower than A	Left, Slower than A	Left, Same speed as A
1	2	3	4	5

4 — If wheel **B** keeps turning clockwise, how does gear **A** turn?

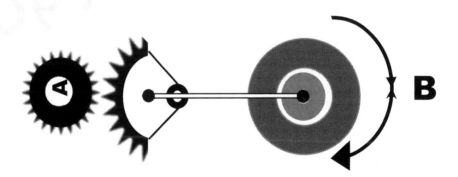

Clockwise	Counter Clockwise	First Clockwise Then Counter clockwise	First Counter Clockwise Then Clockwise
1	2	3	4

5   If wheel **A** turns in clockwise direction, how does wheel **C** turn?

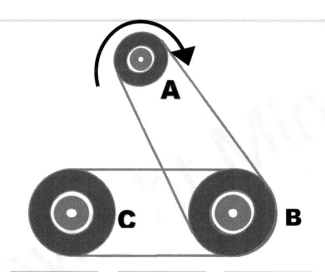

Clockwise, Slower than A	Counter Clockwise, Slower than A	Clockwise, Faster than A	Counter Clockwise, Slower than A	Clockwise, Same speed as A
1	2	3	4	5

6 Surface of three-dimensional cube is laid out flat showing each face of the cube. Which pattern can be folded to make the cube shown?

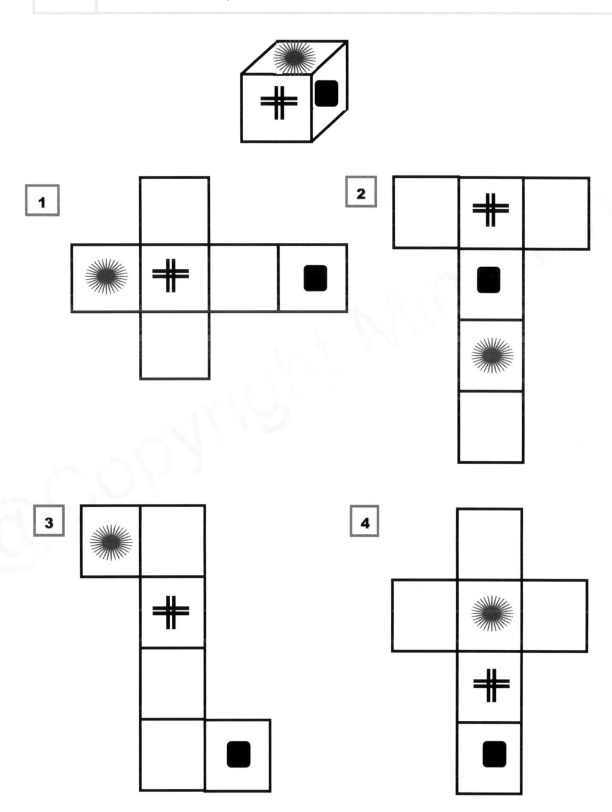

7 Surface of three-dimensional cube is laid out flat showing each face of the cube. Which pattern can be folded to make the cube shown?

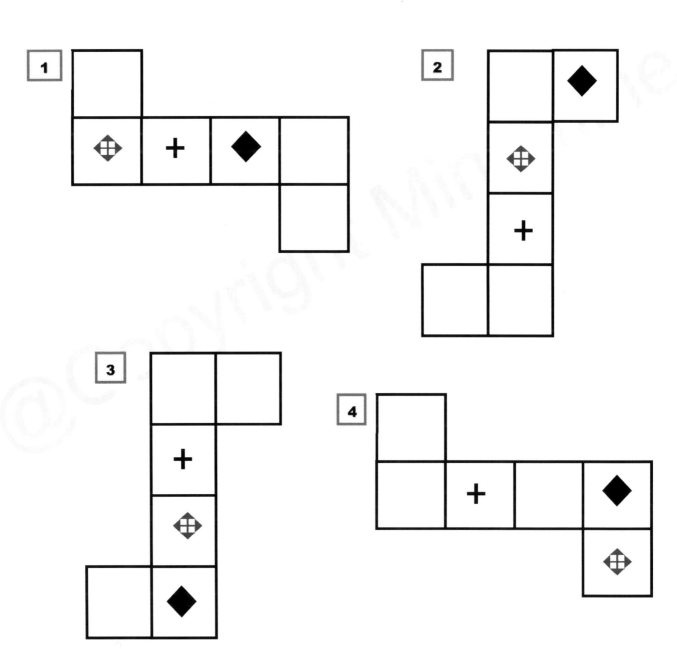

8 Which figure can be assembled using each of the provided pieces?

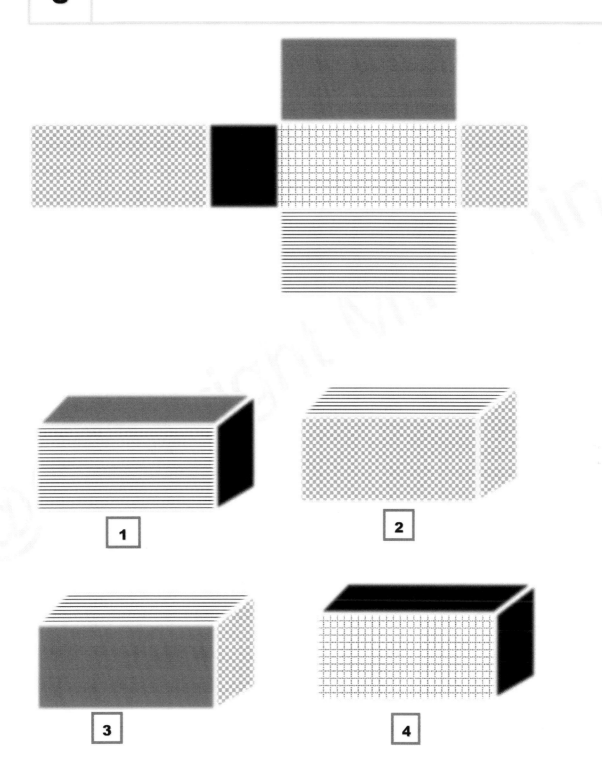

9 A 3-Dimesional Cube is shown below with three different views. Which face is across "A"?

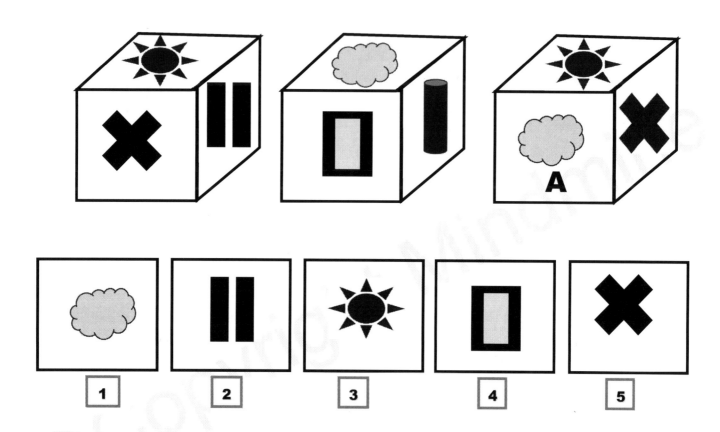

10 A 3-Dimesional Cube is shown below with three different views. Which shape is across "Face A"?

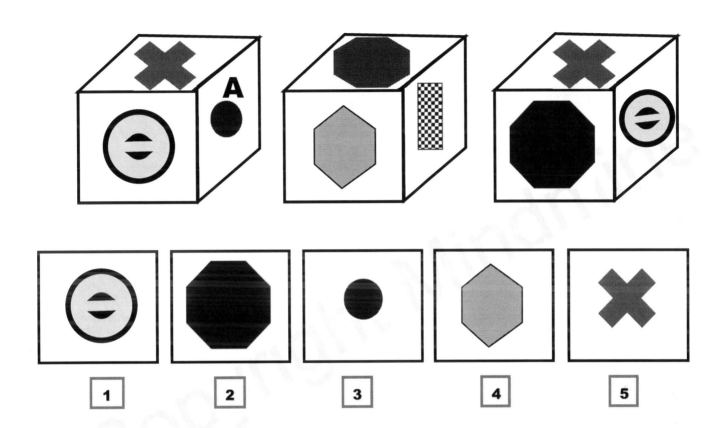

11 Find the answer that exactly matches the below figure when is turned around or rotated

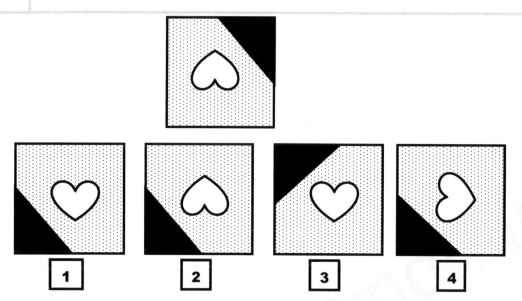

12 Find the answer that exactly matches the below figure when is turned around or rotated

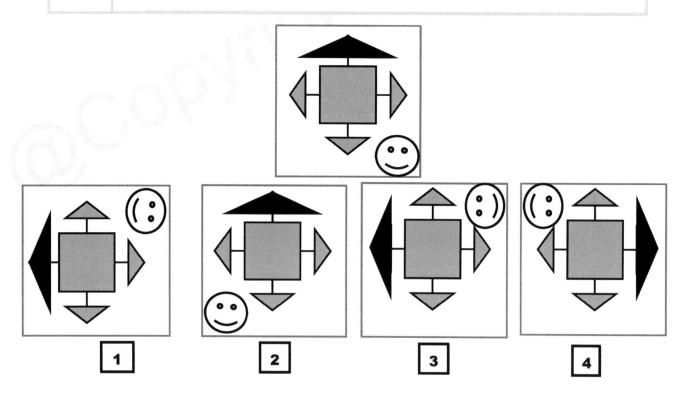

13 Find the answer that exactly matches the below figure when is turned around or rotated

14 Find the answer that exactly matches the below figure when is turned around or rotated

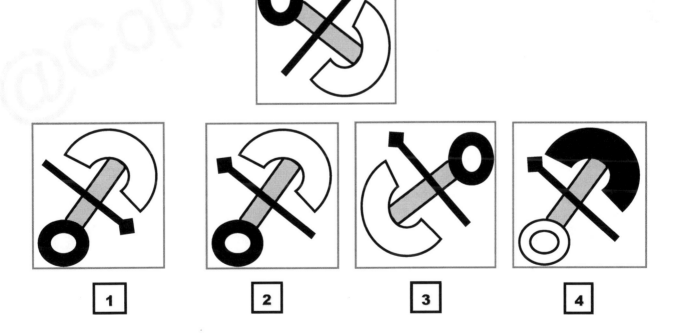

15 Find the answer that exactly matches the below figure when is turned around or rotated

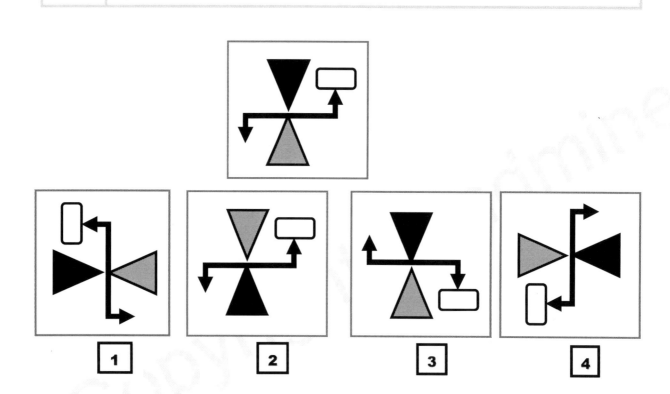

16 A set of figures are arranged in a pattern below. Find the answer that belongs where question mark is?

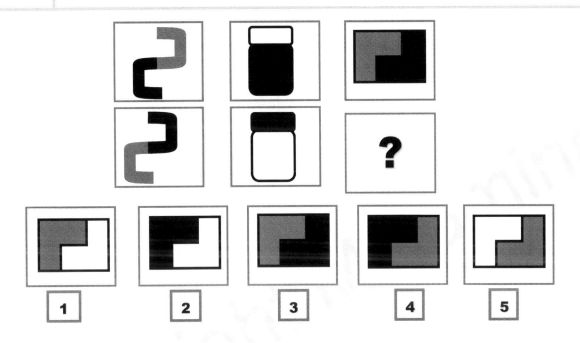

17 A set of figures are arranged in a pattern below. Find the answer that belongs where question mark is?

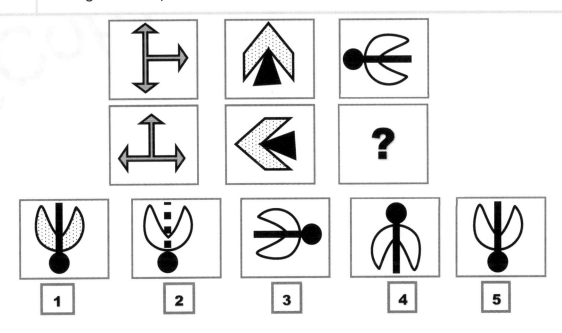

18 — A set of figures are arranged in a pattern below. Find the answer that belongs where question mark is?

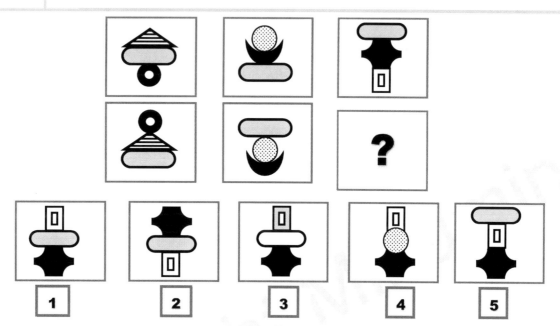

19 — A set of figures are arranged in a pattern below. Find the answer that belongs where question mark is?

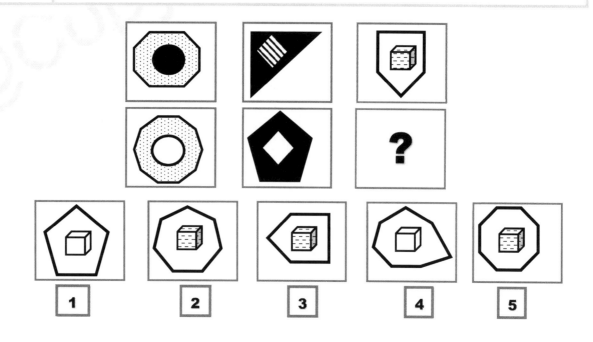

| 20 | A set of figures are arranged in a pattern below. Find the answer that belongs where question mark is? |

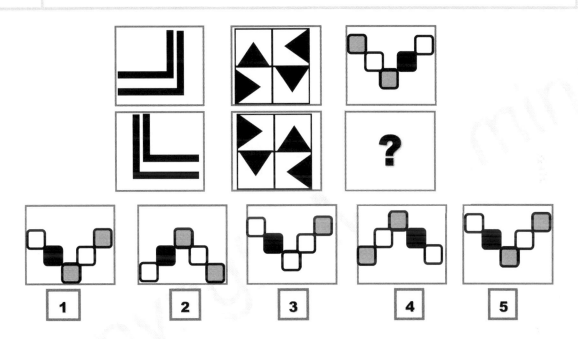

SPATIAL ABILITY

MECHANICAL REASONING

Gears

🗣 A gear is a toothed wheel or Cylinder

🗣 Gears can be connected by belt
🗣 Gear can be meshed (touching each other)

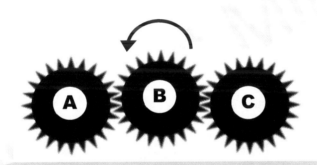

🗣 If gears are touching, adjacent gears move in opposite directions.

Gear "B" is turning in <u>Counter-Clockwise</u> direction.

Gear "A" turns in <u>Clockwise</u> direction.

Gear "C" turns in <u>Clockwise</u> direction.

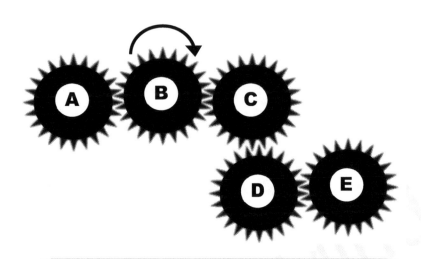

🧠 If gears are touching, adjacent gears move in opposite directions.

Gear "B" is turning in <u>Clockwise</u> direction.

Gear "A" turns in <u>Counter-Clockwise</u> direction.

Gear "C" turns in <u>Counter-Clockwise</u> direction.

Gear "D" turns in <u>Clockwise</u> direction.

Gear "E" turns in <u>Counter-Clockwise</u> direction.

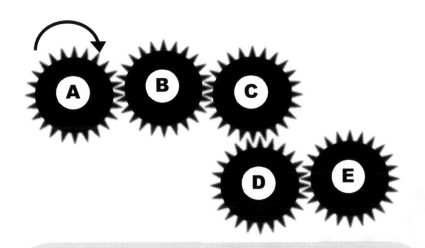

🧠 When there are ODD number of gears, <u>first gear</u> and <u>last gear</u> always turn in the <u>same direction</u>

Gear "A" is turning in <u>Clockwise</u> direction.

Gear "E" turns in <u>Clockwise</u> direction.

*** There are 5 gears in this example ****

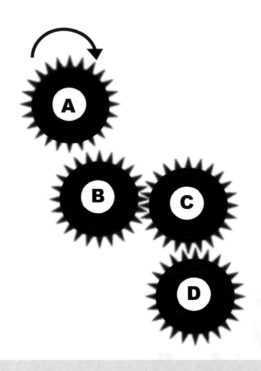

> 🧠 When there are <u>EVEN</u> number of gears, <u>first gear</u> and <u>last gear</u> always turn in the <u>Opposite direction</u>

Gear "A" is turning in <u>Clockwise</u> direction.

Gear "E" turns in <u>Counter-Clockwise</u> direction.

*** There are 4 gears in this example ****

🧠 Gears with <u>equal number of teeth</u> will turn at the same speed. Gear "B", "C" and "D" turn at the same speed

*** They all have equal number of teeth

(all gears are of same size) ***

🧠 If gears have <u>unequal number of teeth,</u> **Smaller gears** will have less teeth and **turn faster**.

Gear "P turn faster than gear Q

*** Gear "P" is smaller than gear "Q" ***

Note: Bar is on the Top, Gear attached to the bottom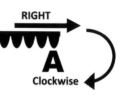

🧠 If Bar moves RIGHT, consider its movement has **Clockwise** turn. **Attached gear turns in the same direction (Clockwise)**

**** Bar moves Right, Gear "P turn Clockwise ***

Note: Bar is on the Bottom, Gear attached to the top

🧠 If Bar moves LEFT, consider its movement has **Clockwise** turn. **Attached gear turns in the same direction (Clockwise)**

**** Bar moves Left, Gear "P turn Clockwise ***

🧠 If Bar moves TOP, consider its movement has **Clockwise** turn. **Attached gear turns in the same direction (Clockwise)**

**** Bar "A moves **TOP** (Clockwise), Gear "P turn Clockwise ***

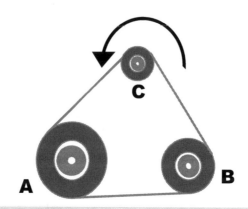

🧠 If gears (or wheels) are connected by a belt, they move in the same direction

Gear "C is turning <u>Counter-Clockwise</u>

Gear "A turns <u>Counter-Clockwise</u>

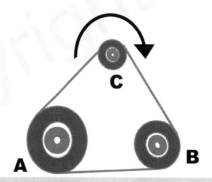

🧠 If gears (or wheels) are connected by a belt, they move in the same direction

Gear "C is turning <u>Clockwise</u>

Gear "A turns <u>Clockwise</u>

1 If gear **A** turns in clockwise direction, how does gear **D** turn?

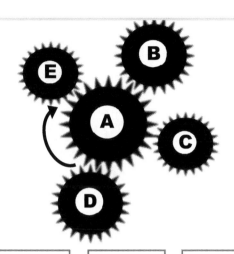

Clockwise, Slower than A	Counter Clockwise, Slower than A	Clockwise, Faster than A	Counter Clockwise, Slower than A	Clockwise, Same speed as A
1	2	3	4	5

2 If gear **A** turns in counter clockwise direction, how does gear **C** turn?

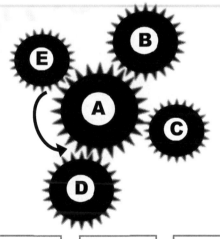

Clockwise, Slower than A	Counter Clockwise, Slower than A	Clockwise, Faster than A	Counter Clockwise, Slower than A	Clockwise, Same speed as A
1	2	3	4	5

3 If gear **C** turns in clockwise direction, how does gear **A** turn?

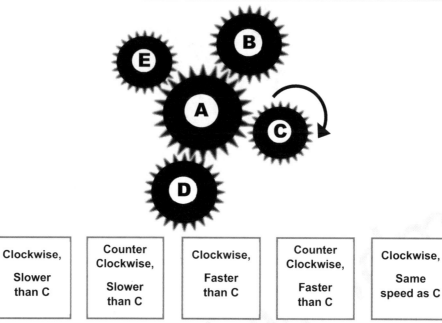

Clockwise, Slower than C	Counter Clockwise, Slower than C	Clockwise, Faster than C	Counter Clockwise, Faster than C	Clockwise, Same speed as C
1	2	3	4	5

4 If gear **C** turns in counter clockwise direction, how does gear **A** turn?

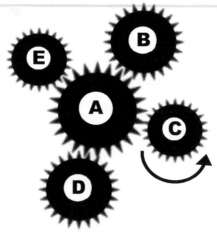

Clockwise, Slower than C	Counter Clockwise, Slower than C	Clockwise, Faster than C	Counter Clockwise, Faster than C	Clockwise, Same speed as C
1	2	3	4	5

5 If gear **A** turns in clockwise direction, how does gear **B** turn?

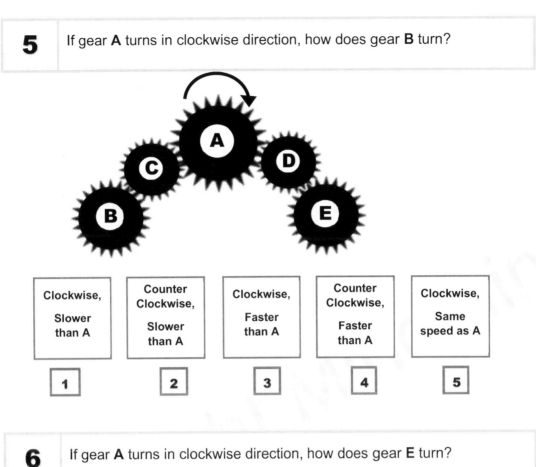

Clockwise, Slower than A	Counter Clockwise, Slower than A	Clockwise, Faster than A	Counter Clockwise, Faster than A	Clockwise, Same speed as A
1	2	3	4	5

6 If gear **A** turns in clockwise direction, how does gear **E** turn?

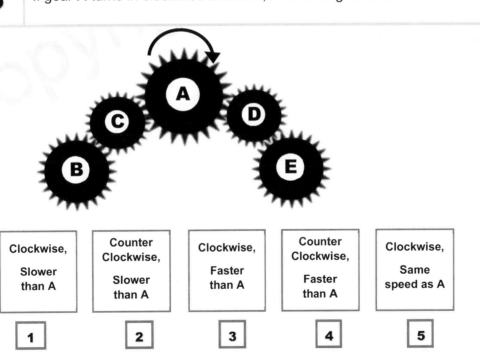

Clockwise, Slower than A	Counter Clockwise, Slower than A	Clockwise, Faster than A	Counter Clockwise, Faster than A	Clockwise, Same speed as A
1	2	3	4	5

| 7 | If gear **A** turns in counter clockwise direction, how does gear **C** turn? |

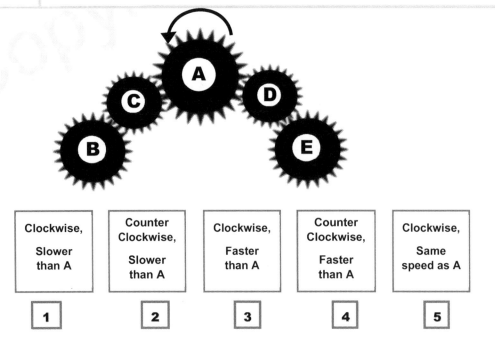

Clockwise, Slower than A	Counter Clockwise, Slower than A	Clockwise, Faster than A	Counter Clockwise, Faster than A	Clockwise, Same speed as A
1	2	3	4	5

| 8 | If gear **A** turns in counter clockwise direction, how does gear **D** turn? |

Clockwise, Slower than A	Counter Clockwise, Slower than A	Clockwise, Faster than A	Counter Clockwise, Faster than A	Clockwise, Same speed as A
1	2	3	4	5

9 If gear **G** turns in counter clockwise direction, how does gear **A** turn?

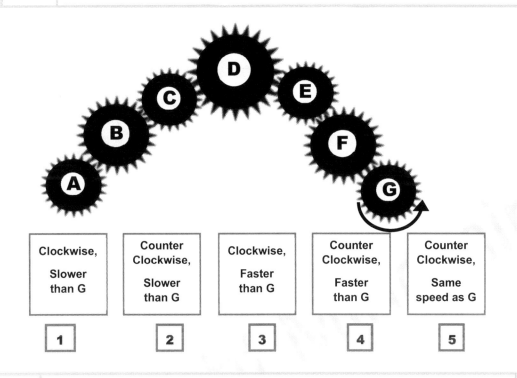

Clockwise, Slower than G	Counter Clockwise, Slower than G	Clockwise, Faster than G	Counter Clockwise, Faster than G	Counter Clockwise, Same speed as G
1	2	3	4	5

10 If gear **A** turns in clockwise direction, how does gear **D** turn?

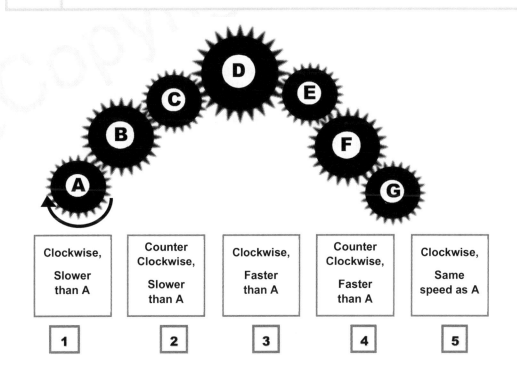

Clockwise, Slower than A	Counter Clockwise, Slower than A	Clockwise, Faster than A	Counter Clockwise, Faster than A	Clockwise, Same speed as A
1	2	3	4	5

11 If gear **D** turns in counter clockwise direction, how does gear **A** turn?

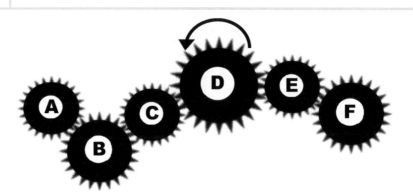

Clockwise, Slower than D	Counter Clockwise, Slower than D	Clockwise, Faster than D	Counter Clockwise, Faster than D	Counter Clockwise, Same speed as D
1	2	3	4	5

12 If gear **1** turns in counter clockwise direction, how does gear **4** turn?

Clockwise, Slower than 1	Counter Clockwise, Slower than 1	Clockwise, Faster than 1	Counter Clockwise, Faster than 1	Counter Clockwise, Same speed as 1
1	2	3	4	5

13 If gear **I** turns in counter clockwise direction, how does gear **E** turn?

Clockwise, Slower than I	Counter Clockwise, Slower than I	Clockwise, Faster than I	Counter Clockwise, Faster than I	Counter Clockwise, Same speed as I
1	2	3	4	5

14 If gear **A** turns in counter clockwise direction, how does gear **C** turn?

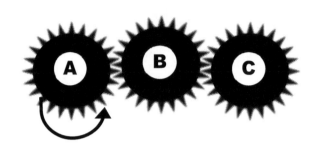

Clockwise, Slower than A	Counter Clockwise, Slower than A	Clockwise, Faster than A	Counter Clockwise, Faster than A	Counter Clockwise, Same speed as A
1	2	3	4	5

15 If gear **A** turns in clockwise direction, how does gear **C** turn?

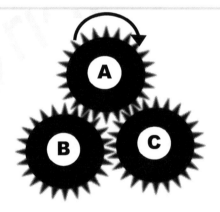

Clockwise, Slower than A	Counter Clockwise, Slower than A	Clockwise, Faster than A	Counter Clockwise, Faster than A	Counter Clockwise, Same speed as A
1	2	3	4	5

16 If gear **A** turns in clockwise direction, how does gear **B** turn?

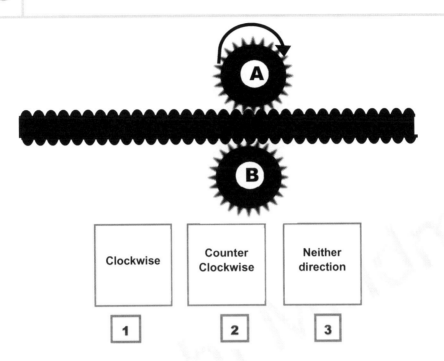

Clockwise	Counter Clockwise	Neither direction
1	2	3

17 If **X** moves left, how does gears turn?

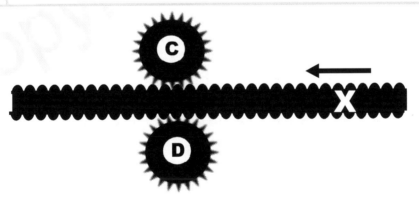

Both Clockwise	Both Clockwise	C- Clockwise, D- Counter Clockwise	D- Clockwise, C- Counter Clockwise	Neither direction
1	2	3	4	5

18 If **X** moves right, how does gears turn?

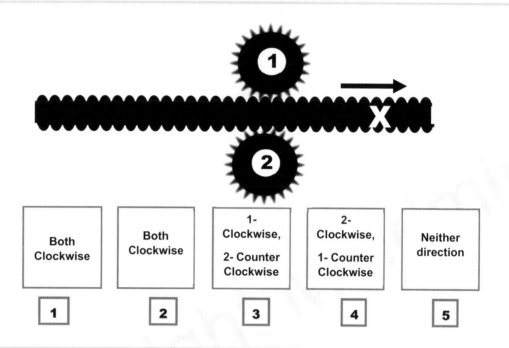

Both Clockwise	Both Clockwise	1- Clockwise, 2- Counter Clockwise	2- Clockwise, 1- Counter Clockwise	Neither direction
1	2	3	4	5

19 If gear **2** turns in clockwise direction, how does gear **1** turn?

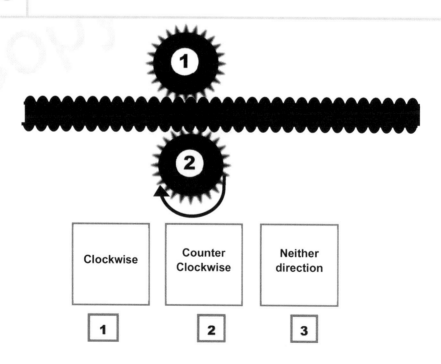

Clockwise	Counter Clockwise	Neither direction
1	2	3

20 If bar **A** moves right at a steady speed, how does bar B turn?

Right, Faster than A	Left, Faster than A	Right, Slower than A	Left, Slower than A	Left, Same speed as A
1	2	3	4	5

21 If bar **A** moves left at a steady speed, how does bar B turn?

Right, Faster than A	Left, Faster than A	Right, Slower than A	Left, Slower than A	Left, Same speed as A
1	2	3	4	5

22 If bar **1** moves left at a steady speed, how does bar 2 turn?

Right, Faster than 1	Left, Faster than 1	Right, Slower than 1	Left, Slower than 1	Left, Same speed as 1
1	2	3	4	5

23 If bar **1** moves left at a steady speed, how does bar 2 turn?

Right, Faster than 1	Left, Faster than 1	Right, Slower than 1	Left, Slower than 1	Left, Same speed as 1
1	2	3	4	5

24 If wheel **X** keeps turning clockwise, how does gear **A** turn?

1	2	3	4
Clockwise	Counter Clockwise	First Clockwise Then Counter clockwise	First Counter Clockwise Then Clockwise

| **25** | If wheel **X** keeps turning counter clockwise, how does gear **A** turn? |

Clockwise	Counter Clockwise	First Clockwise Then Counter clockwise	First Counter Clockwise Then Clockwise
1	2	3	4

26 If wheel **X** keeps turning counter clockwise, how does gear **A** turn?

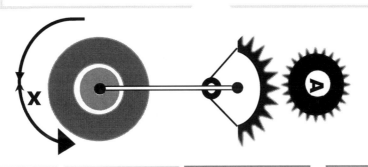

Clockwise	Counter Clockwise	First Clockwise Then Counter clockwise	First Counter Clockwise Then Clockwise
1	2	3	4

27 If wheel **X** keeps turning clockwise, how does gear **Y** turn?

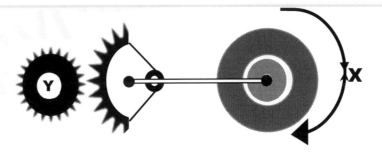

Clockwise	Counter Clockwise	First Clockwise Then Counter clockwise	First Counter Clockwise Then Clockwise
1	2	3	4

28 If wheel **X** keeps turning counter clockwise, how does gear **A** turn?

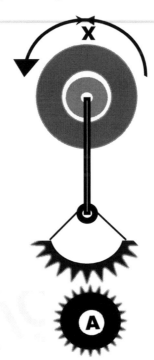

Clockwise	Counter Clockwise	First Clockwise Then Counter clockwise	First Counter Clockwise Then Clockwise
1	2	3	4

29 If wheel **A** turns in counter clockwise direction, how does wheel **B** turn?

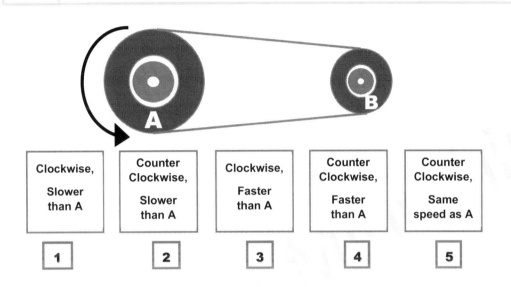

30 If wheel **A** turns in clockwise direction, how does wheel **B** turn?

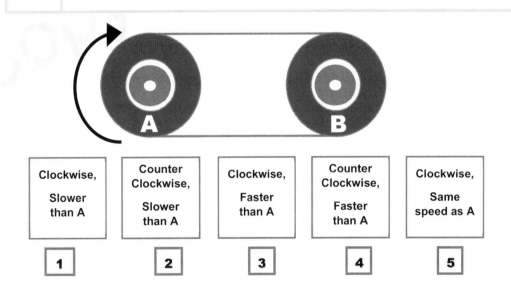

31 If wheel **A** turns in clockwise direction, how does wheel **C** turn?

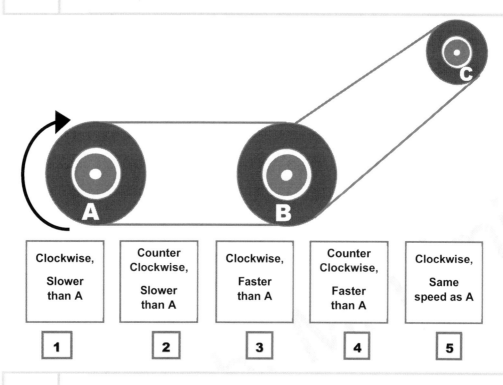

Clockwise, Slower than A	Counter Clockwise, Slower than A	Clockwise, Faster than A	Counter Clockwise, Faster than A	Clockwise, Same speed as A
1	2	3	4	5

32 If wheel **C** turns in clockwise direction, how does wheel **B** turn?

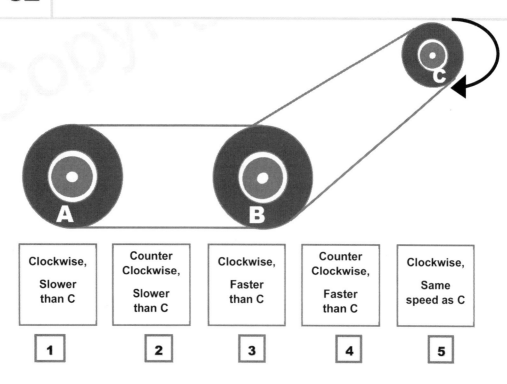

Clockwise, Slower than C	Counter Clockwise, Slower than C	Clockwise, Faster than C	Counter Clockwise, Faster than C	Clockwise, Same speed as C
1	2	3	4	5

33 If wheel **C** turns in counter clockwise direction, how does wheel **B** turn?

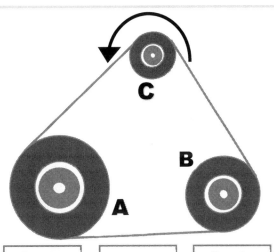

Clockwise, Slower than C	Counter Clockwise, Slower than C	Clockwise, Faster than C	Counter Clockwise, Faster than C	Clockwise, Same speed as C
1	2	3	4	5

34 If wheel **B** turns in counter clockwise direction, how does wheel **C** turn?

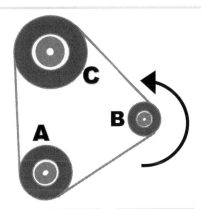

Clockwise, Slower than B	Counter Clockwise, Slower than B	Clockwise, Faster than B	Counter Clockwise, Faster than B	Clockwise, Same speed as B
1	2	3	4	5

35 If wheel **A** turns in clockwise direction, how does wheel **C** turn?

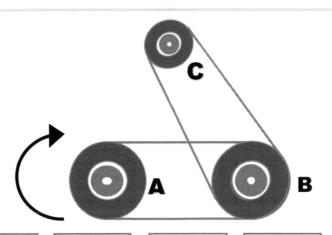

Clockwise, Slower than A	Counter Clockwise, Slower than A	Clockwise, Faster than A	Counter Clockwise, Faster than A	Clockwise, Same speed as A
1	2	3	4	5

36 If wheel **A** turns in clockwise direction, how does wheel **C** turn?

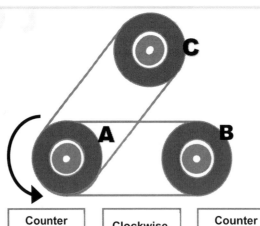

Clockwise, Slower than A	Counter Clockwise, Slower than A	Clockwise, Faster than A	Counter Clockwise, Faster than A	Clockwise, Same speed as A
1	2	3	4	5

37 If wheel **A** turns in counter clockwise direction, how does wheel **C** turn?

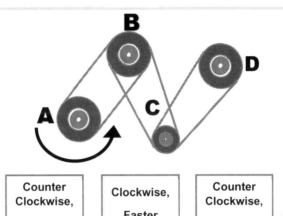

Clockwise, Slower than A	Counter Clockwise, Slower than A	Clockwise, Faster than A	Counter Clockwise, Faster than A	Clockwise, Same speed as A
1	2	3	4	5

38 If wheel **C** turns in counter clockwise direction, how does wheel **D** turn?

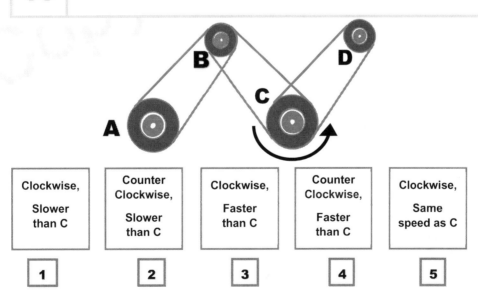

Clockwise, Slower than C	Counter Clockwise, Slower than C	Clockwise, Faster than C	Counter Clockwise, Faster than C	Clockwise, Same speed as C
1	2	3	4	5

39 If wheel **B** turns in counter clockwise direction, how does wheel **C** turn?

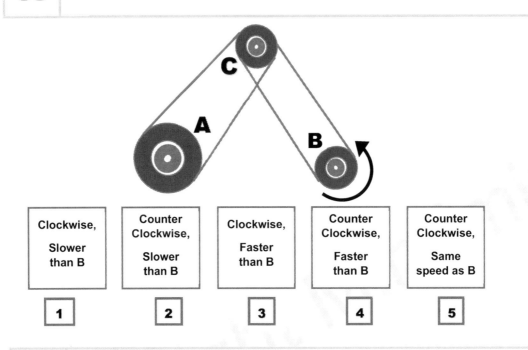

Clockwise, Slower than B	Counter Clockwise, Slower than B	Clockwise, Faster than B	Counter Clockwise, Faster than B	Counter Clockwise, Same speed as B
1	2	3	4	5

40 If wheel **A** turns in clockwise direction, how does wheel **E** turn?

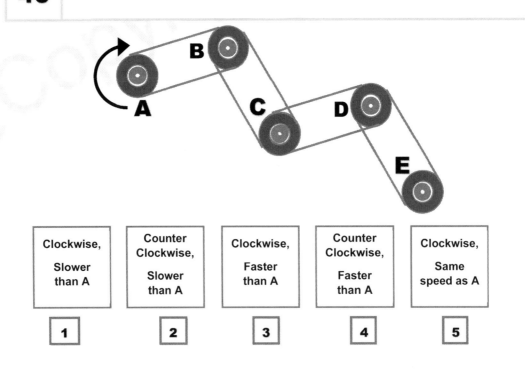

Clockwise, Slower than A	Counter Clockwise, Slower than A	Clockwise, Faster than A	Counter Clockwise, Faster than A	Clockwise, Same speed as A
1	2	3	4	5

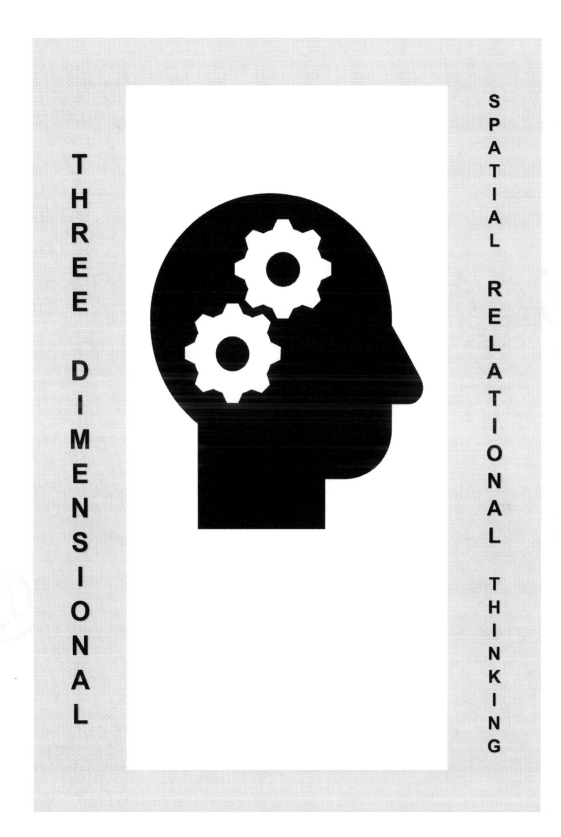

Nets of 3-D Figures

Eleven nets of a Cube

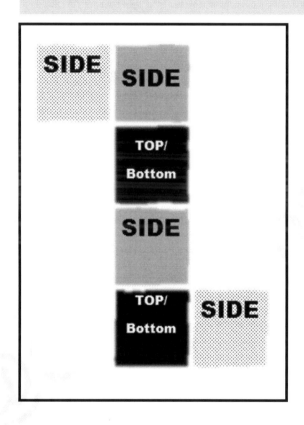
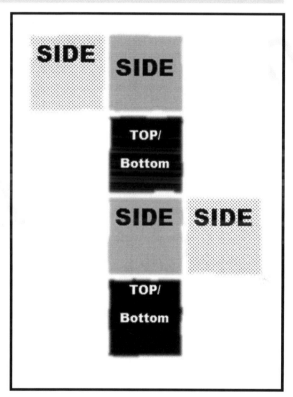

Eleven nets of a Cube

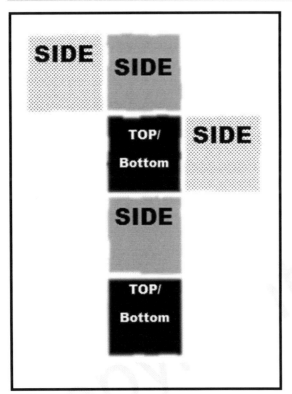
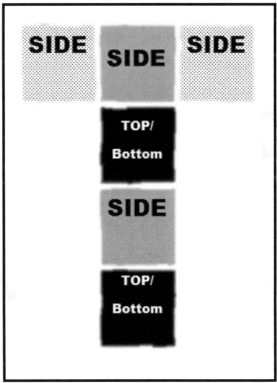

Eleven nets of a Cube

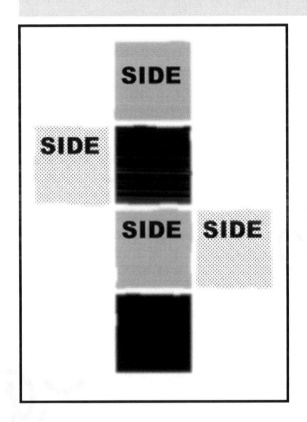
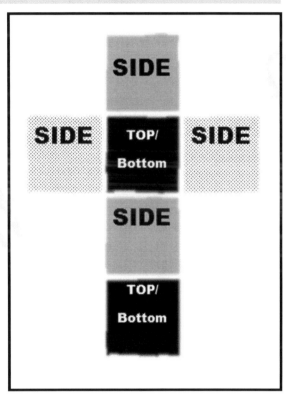

Eleven nets of a Cube

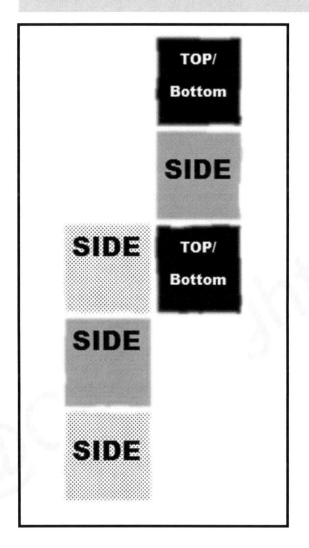
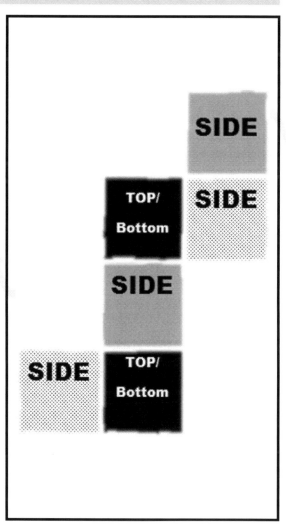

Eleven nets of a Cube

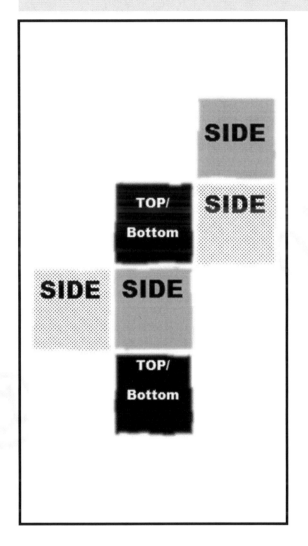
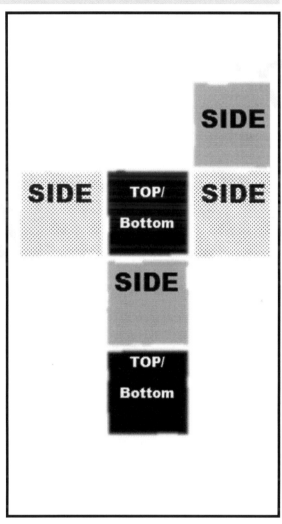

Eleven nets of a Cube

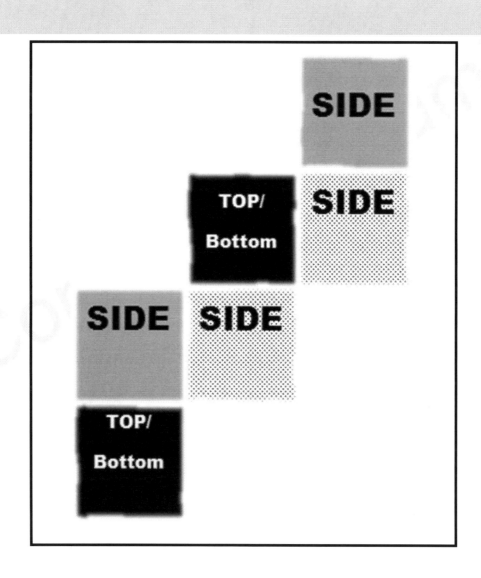

Net of a Square Pyramid	Net of a Rectangular Prism
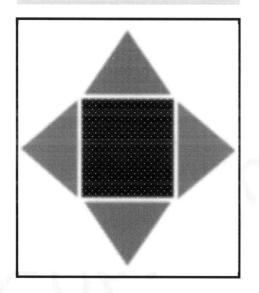	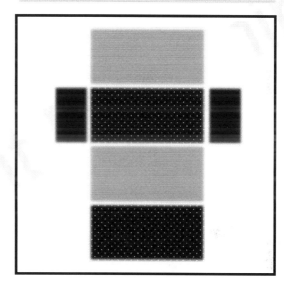

Net of a Triangular Pyramid	Net of a Triangular Prism
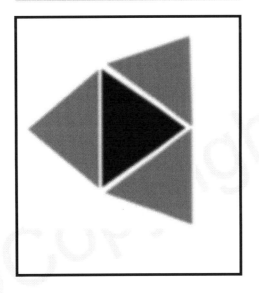	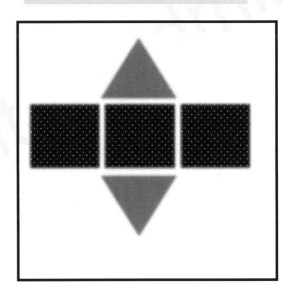

Net of a Pentagonal Pyramid

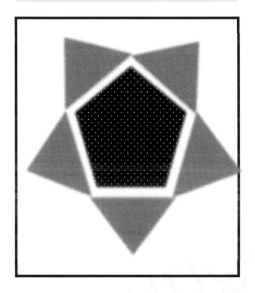

Net of a Hexagonal Prism

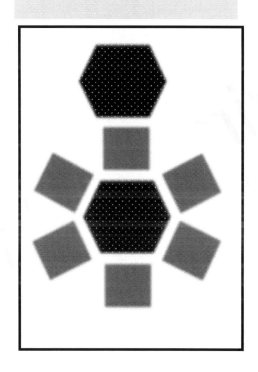

Visualizing a 3-Dimensional cube

A 3-Dimesional Cube is shown below with three different views. Which face is across "A"?

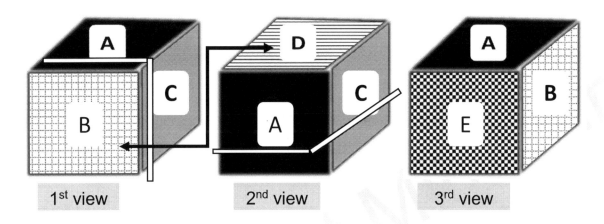

| 1st view | 2nd view | 3rd view |

Elimination Technique: If you see a face on a specific view, they cannot come across.

In the 1st view- B and C are visible. B and C cannot be across A

In the 3rd view- B and E are visible. B and E cannot be across A

*** Eliminate B, C, E ***

Shared Edges Technique:

D has edges shared with A & C.

B has edges shared with A & C.

*** B comes across D ****

B & D cannot be across A. Eliminate D.

Which face is across "A"?

Answer is: Other face not shown in 3 given views (NOT A,B,C,D,E)

Visualizing a 3-Dimensional cube

A 3-Dimesional Cube is shown below with three different views. Which face is across "B"?

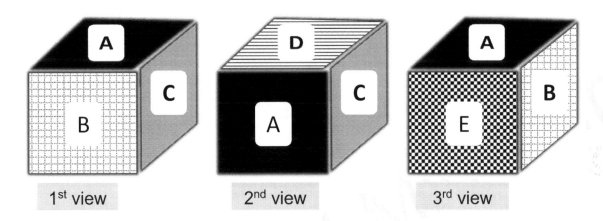

1st view   2nd view   3rd view

Elimination Technique: If you see a face on a specific view, they cannot come across.

In the 1st view- A and C are visible. A and C cannot be across B

In the 3rd view- A and E are visible. A and E cannot be across B

*** Eliminate A, C, E ***

Shared Edges Technique:

D has edges shared with A & C.

B has edges shared with A & C.

*** D comes across B ****

Which face is across "B"?

Answer is: D

Visualizing a 3-Dimensional cube

A 3-Dimesional Cube is shown below with three different views. Which face is across "C"?

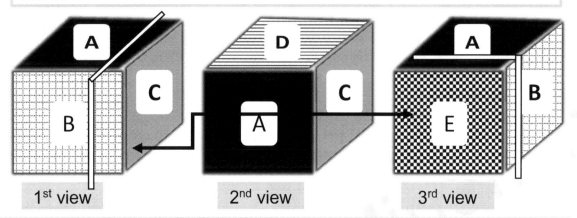

1st view   2nd view   3rd view

Elimination Technique: If you see a face on a specific view, they cannot come across.

In the 1st view- A and B are visible. A and B cannot be across C

In the 2ND view- A and D are visible. A and D cannot be across C

*** Eliminate A, B, D ***

Shared Edges Technique:

B has edges shared with A & C.

B has edges shared with A & E.

*** C comes across E ****.

Rotation Technique:

3rd view comes when 1st view rotated counter clockwise,

*** E comes across C ****.

Which face is across "C"?

Answer is: E

| 41 | A 3-Dimesional Cube is shown below with three different views. Which face is across "A"? |

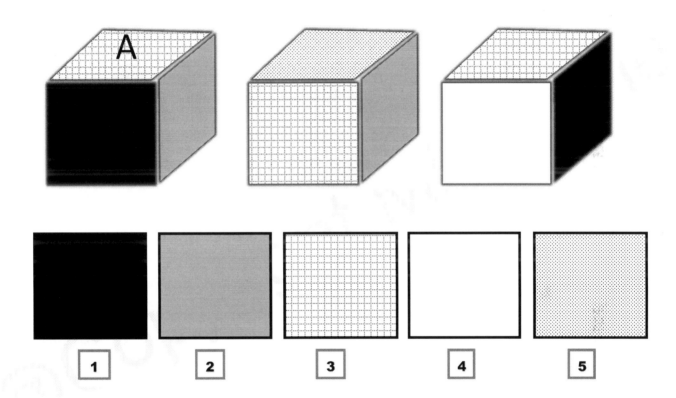

42 A 3-Dimesional Cube is shown below with three different views. Which face is across "A"?

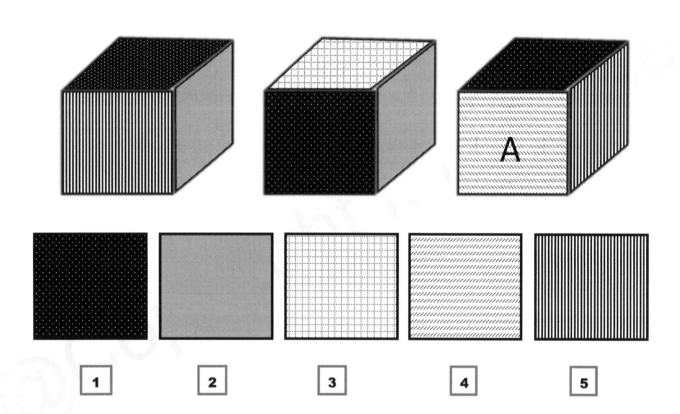

43 A 3-Dimesional Cube is shown below with three different views. Which face is across "A"?

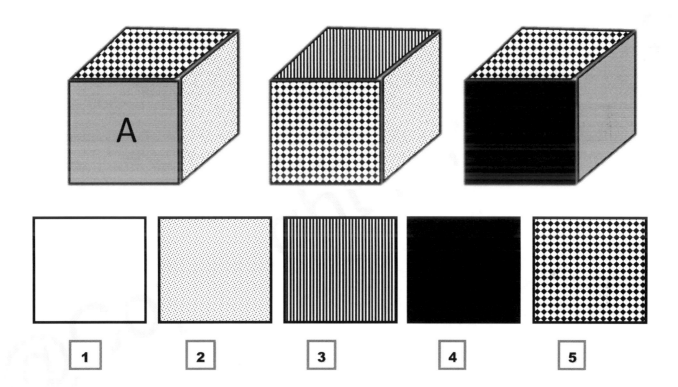

44 A 3-Dimesional Cube is shown below with three different views. Which face is across "A"?

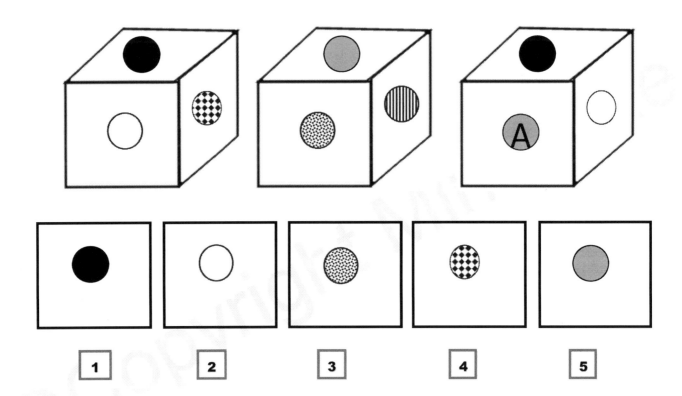

45 A 3-Dimesional Cube is shown below with three different views. Which face is across "A"?

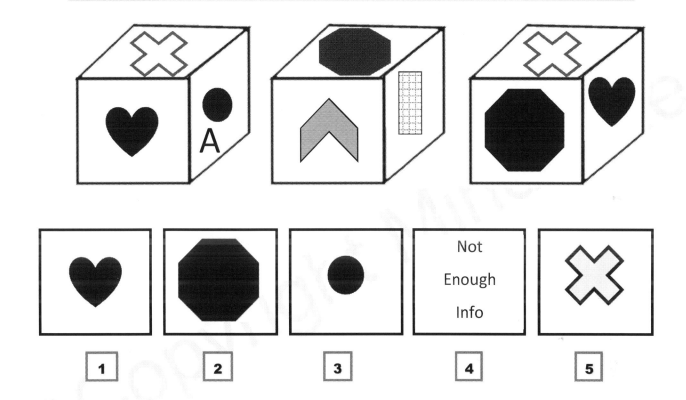

46 A 3-Dimesional Cube is shown below with three different views. Which face is across "A"?

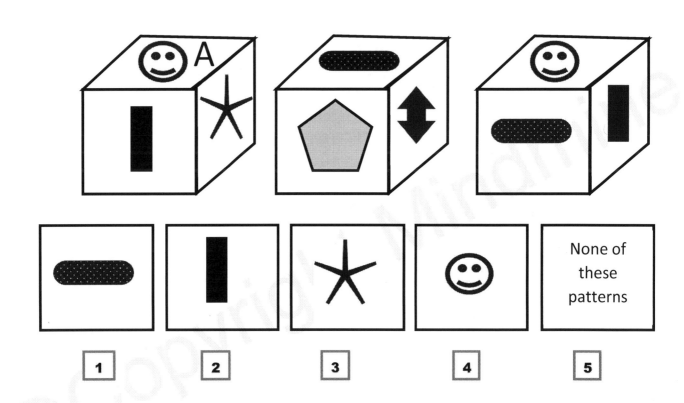

47 A 3-Dimesional Cube is shown below with three different views. Which face is across "A"?

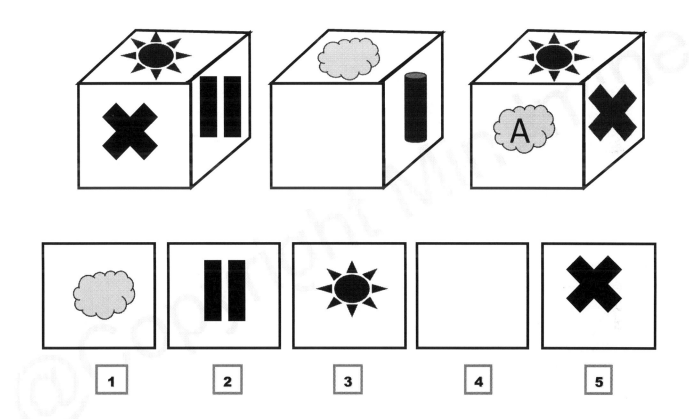

48 A 3-Dimesional Cube is shown below with three different views. Which face is across "A"?

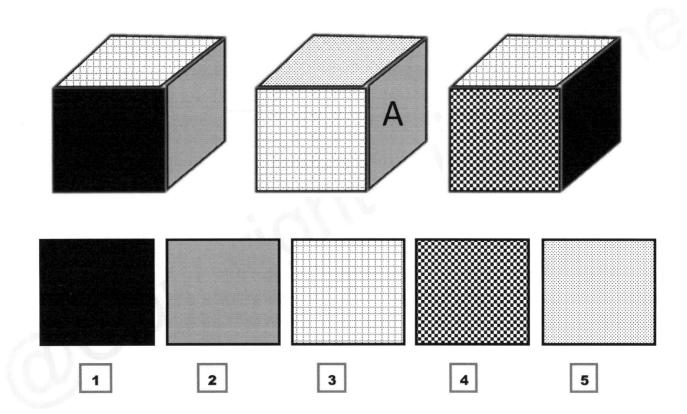

49 A 3-Dimesional Cube is shown below with three different views. Which face is across "A"?

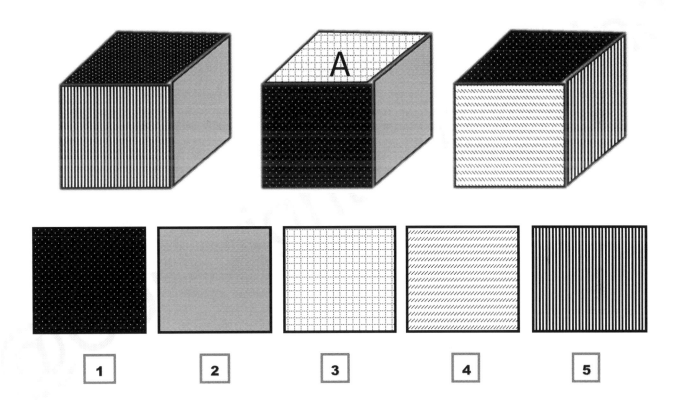

50 A 3-Dimesional Cube is shown below with three different views. Which face is across "A"?

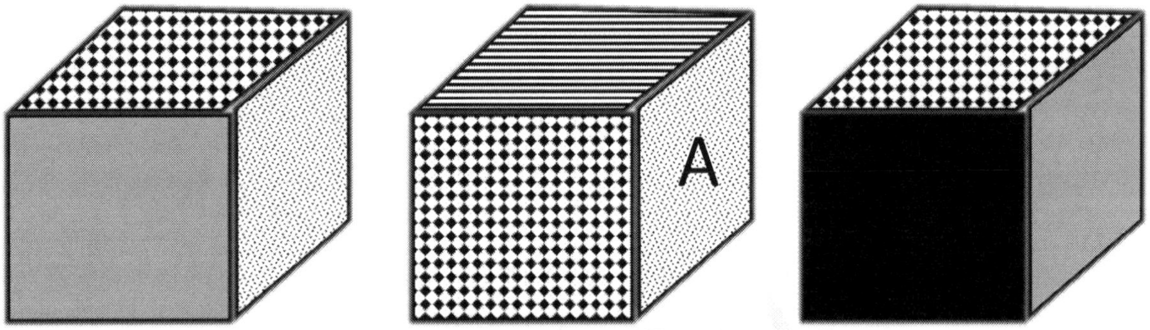

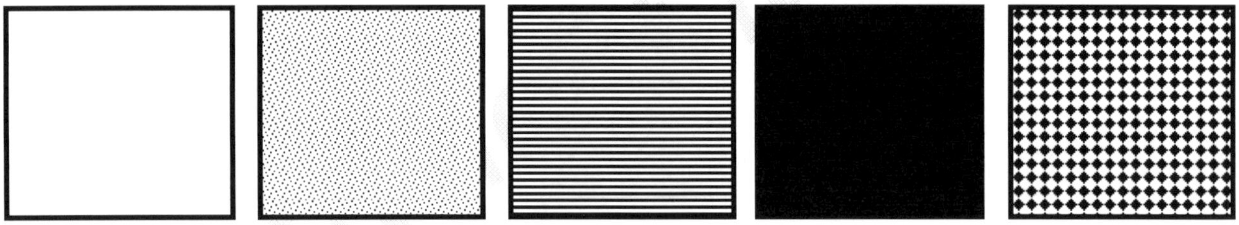

51 A 3-Dimesional Cube is shown below with three different views. Which face is across "A"?

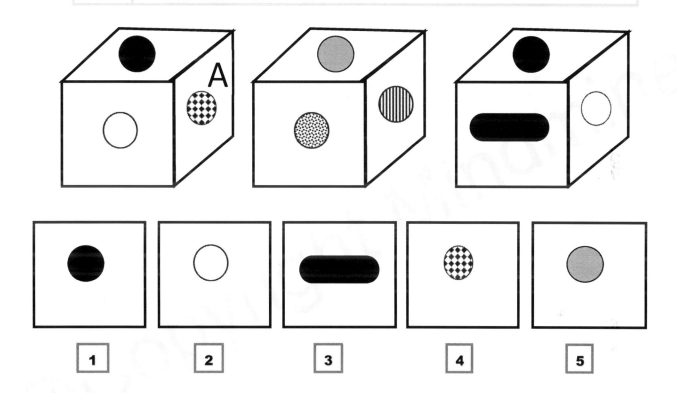

52 A 3-Dimesional Cube is shown below with three different views. Which face is across "A"?

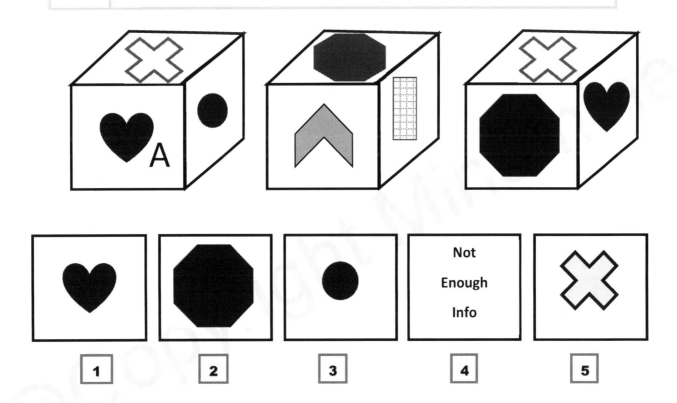

53 A 3-Dimesional Cube is shown below with three different views. Which face is across "A"?

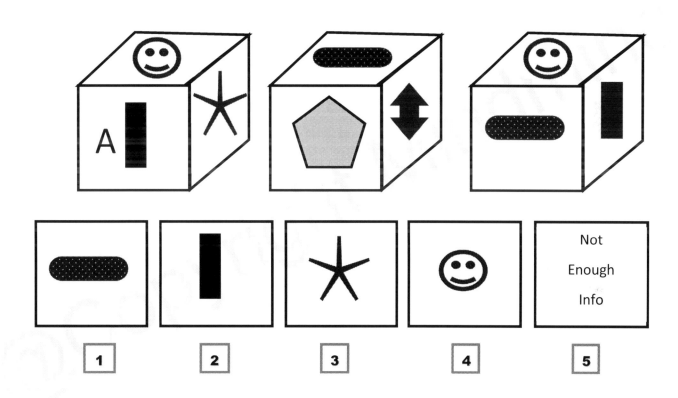

54 A 3-Dimesional Cube is shown below with three different views. Which face is across "A"?

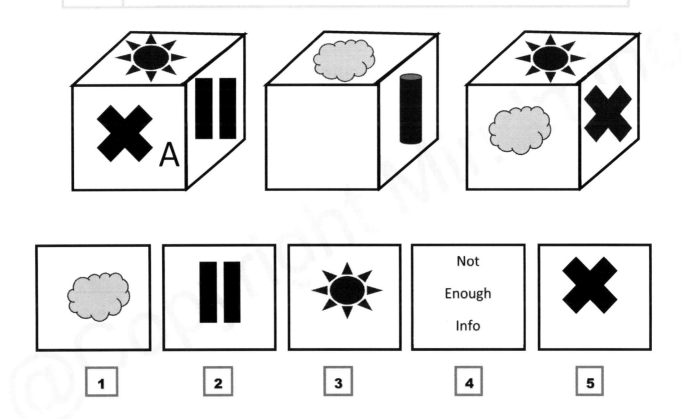

55 A 3-Dimesional Cube is shown below with three different views. Which face comes across "A"?

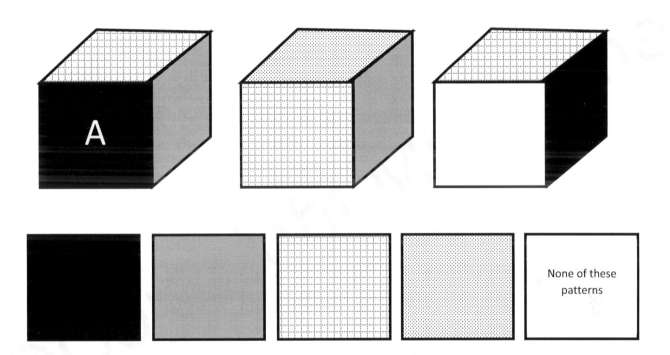

56 A 3-Dimesional Cube is shown below with three different views. Which face is across "A"?

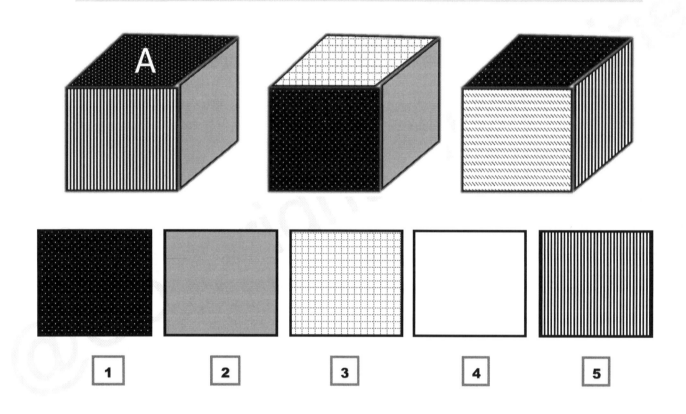

57 A 3-Dimesional Cube is shown below with three different views. Which face is across "A"?

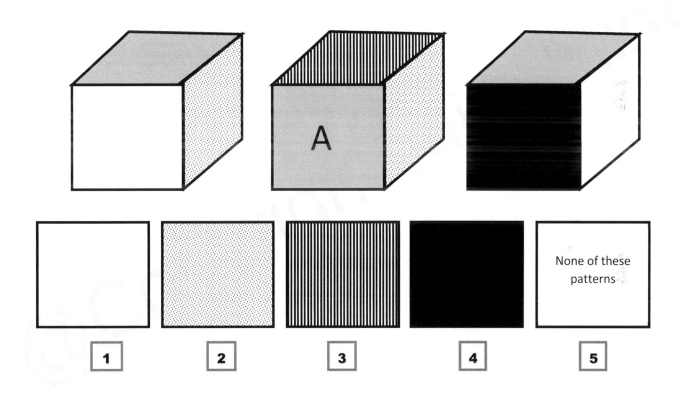

58 A 3-Dimesional Cube is shown below with three different views. Which face is across "A"?

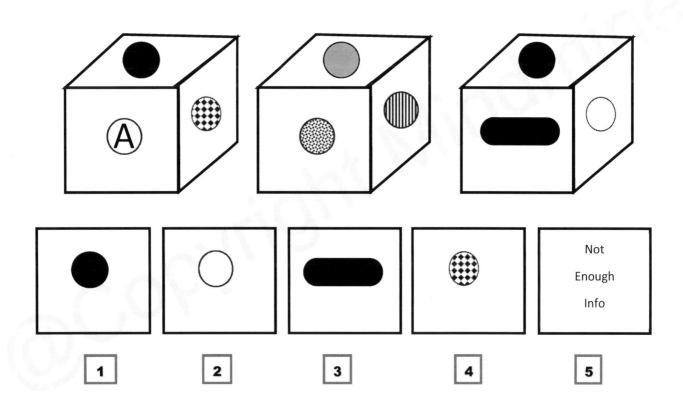

59 A 3-Dimesional Cube is shown below with three different views. Which face is across "A"?

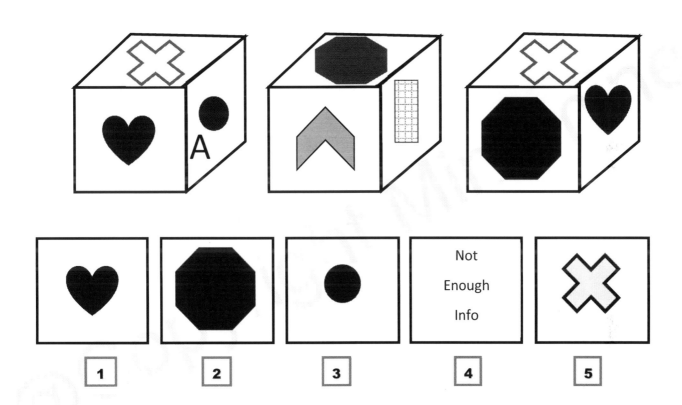

60 A 3-Dimesional Cube is shown below with three different views. Which face is across "A"?

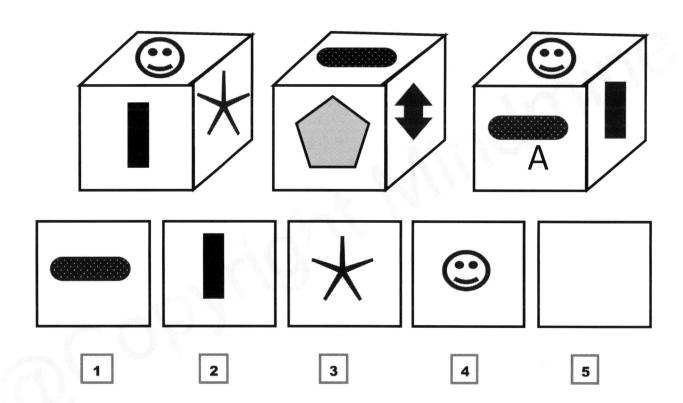

Visualizing nets for 3-Dimensional solid

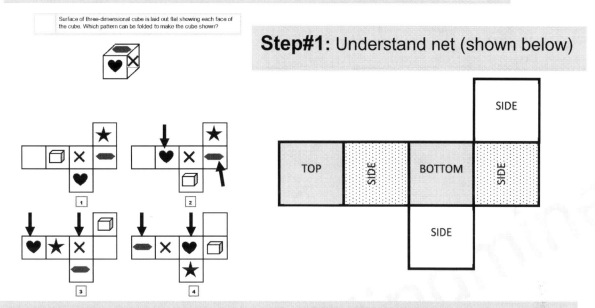

Step#1: Understand net (shown below)

Step#2: Faces shown in the given view, CANNOT come across. Below 3 shapes cannot be across each other

Step#3: Eliminate wrong options:

Option 2 is Incorrect. ⬢ ♥ Shapes are across each other (Sides across each other)

Option 3 is Incorrect. ♥ ✗ Shapes are across each other (Top & Bottom across each other)

Option 4 is Incorrect. ⬢ ♥ Shapes are across each other (Top & Bottom across each other)

Answer is Option 1

61 Surface of three-dimensional cube is laid out flat showing each face of the cube. Which pattern can be folded to make the cube shown?

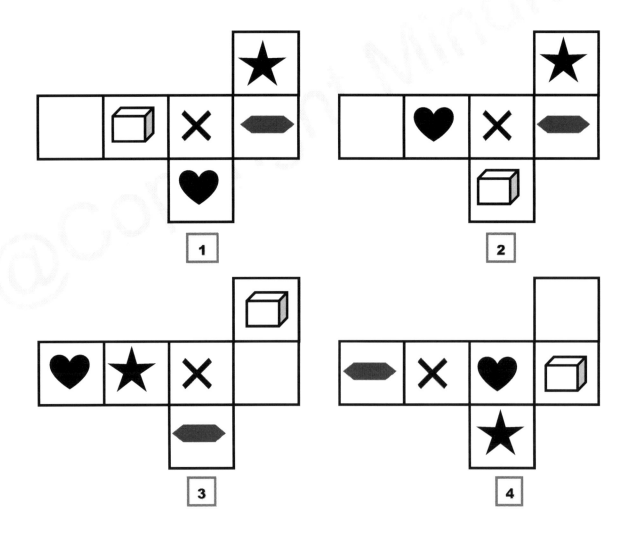

62 Surface of three-dimensional cube is laid out flat showing each face of the cube. Which pattern can be folded to make the cube shown?

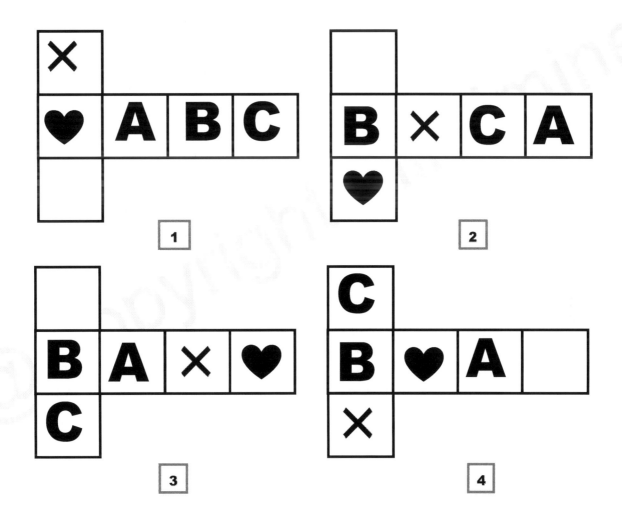

63 Surface of three-dimensional cube is laid out flat showing each face of the cube. Which pattern can be folded to make the cube shown?

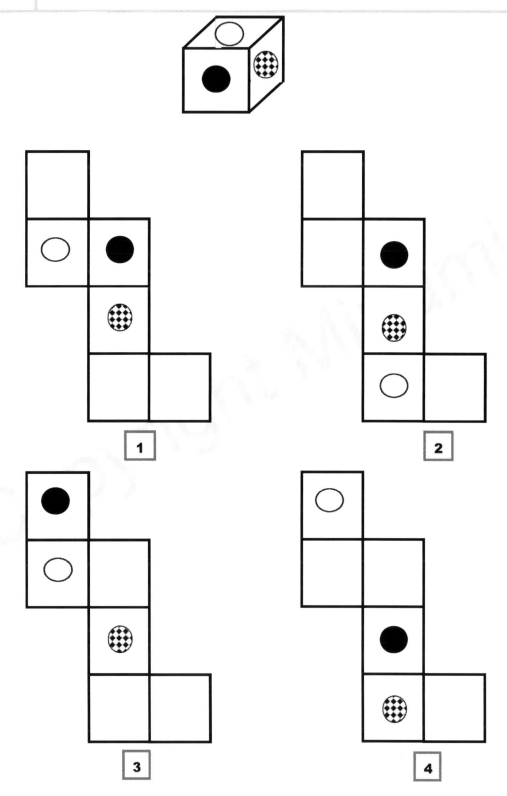

64 Surface of three-dimensional cube is laid out flat showing each face of the cube. Which pattern can be folded to make the cube shown?

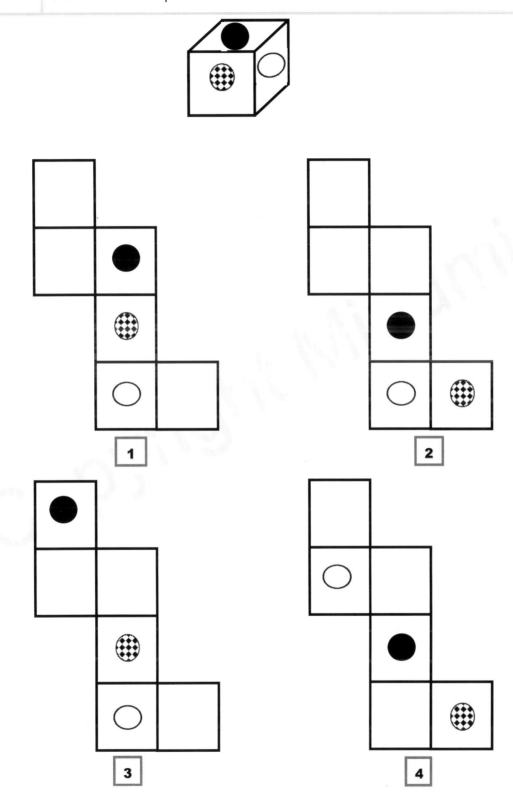

65 Surface of three-dimensional cube is laid out flat showing each face of the cube. Which pattern can be folded to make the cube shown?

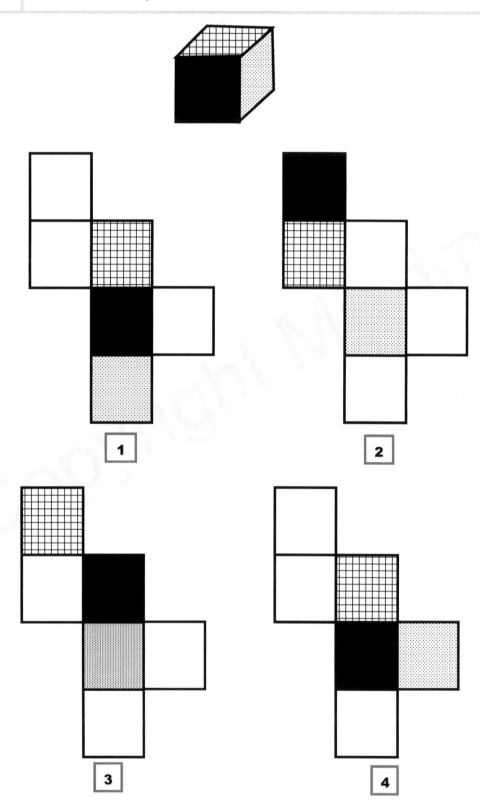

86

66 Surface of three-dimensional cube is laid out flat showing each face of the cube. Which pattern can be folded to make the cube shown?

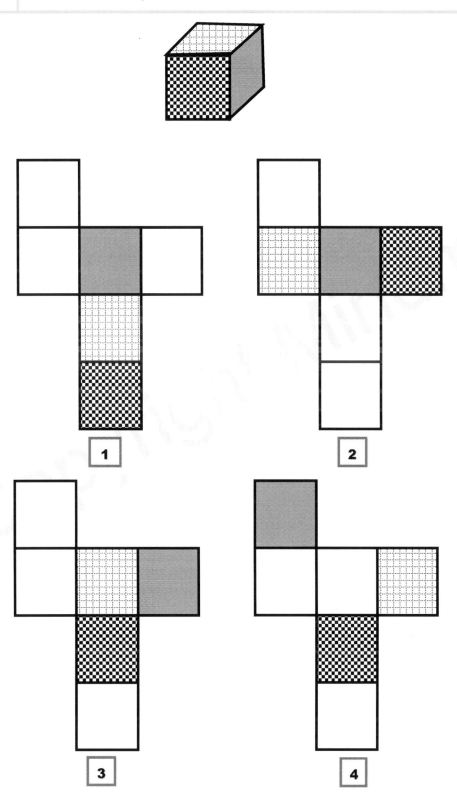

67 Surface of three-dimensional cube is laid out flat showing each face of the cube. Which pattern can be folded to make the cube shown?

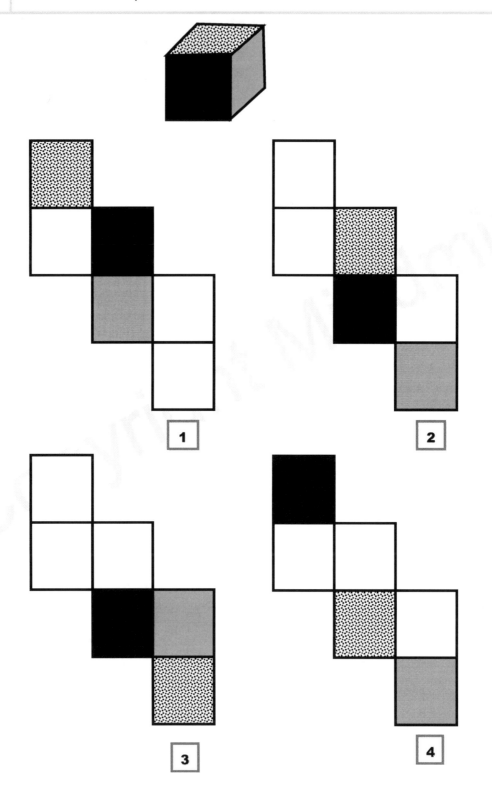

68 Surface of three-dimensional cube is laid out flat showing each face of the cube. Which pattern can be folded to make the cube shown?

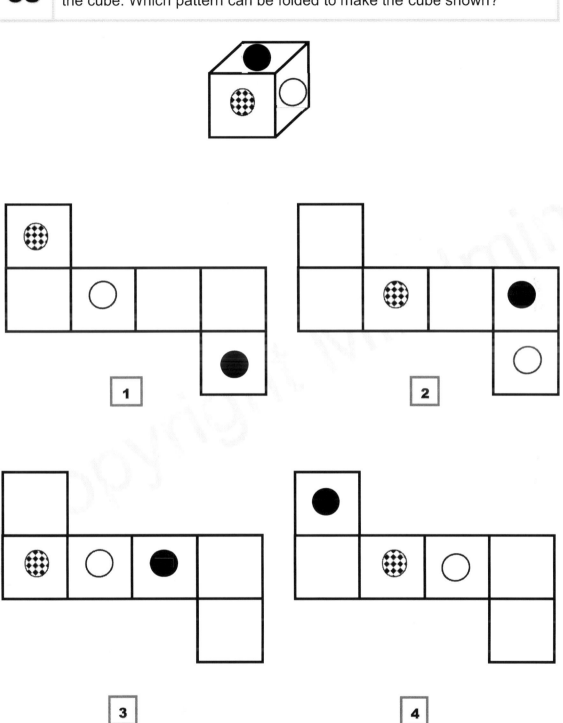

69 Surface of three-dimensional cube is laid out flat showing each face of the cube. Which pattern can be folded to make the cube shown?

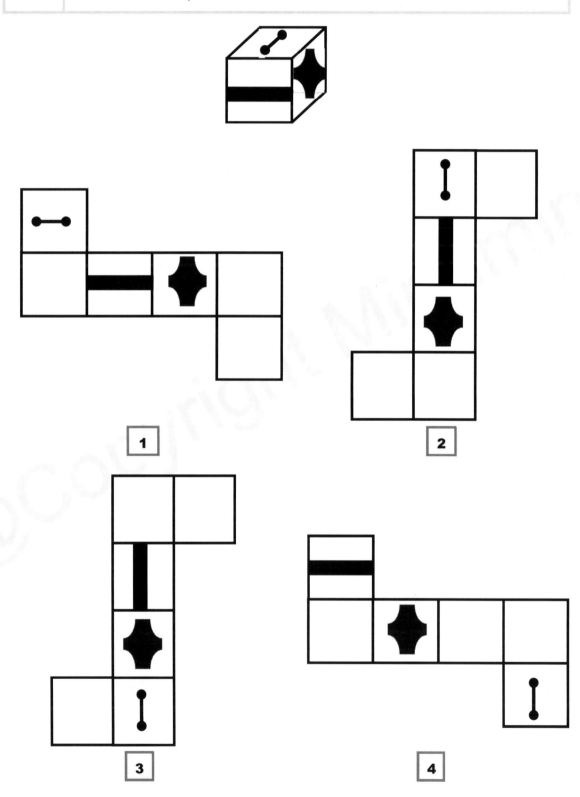

70 Surface of three-dimensional cube is laid out flat showing each face of the cube. Which pattern can be folded to make the cube shown?

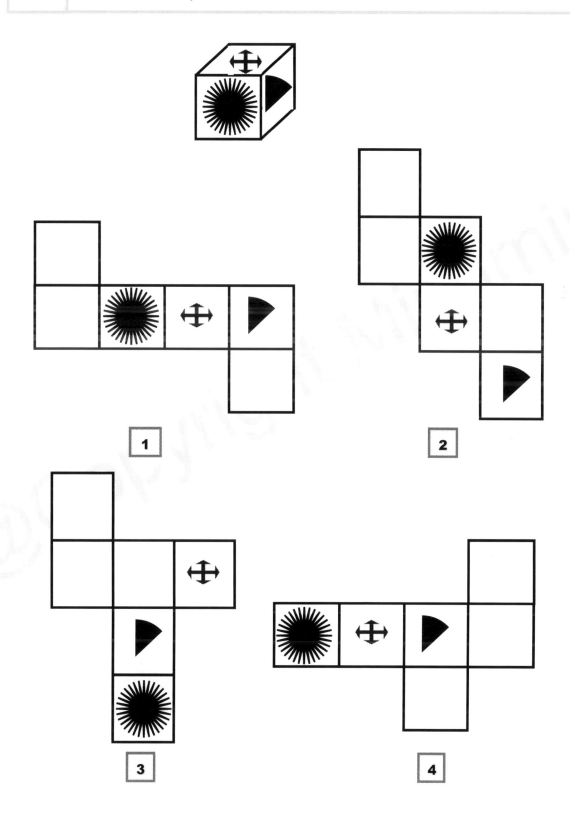

71 Which figure can be assembled using each of the provided pieces?

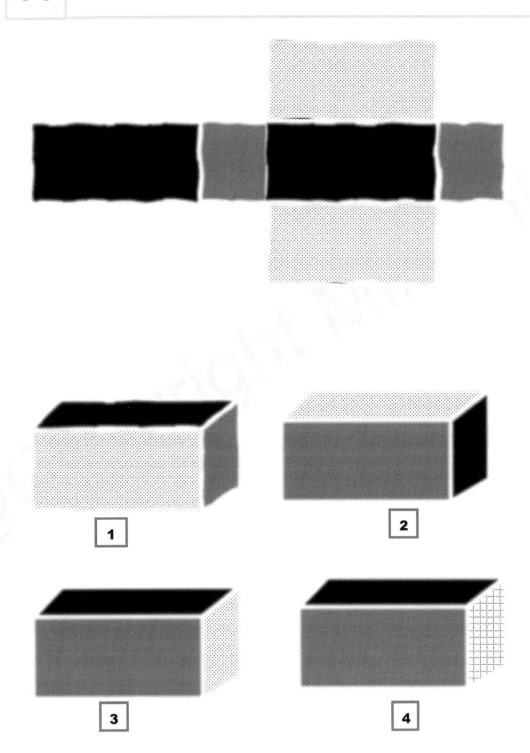

72 Which figure can be assembled using each of the provided pieces?

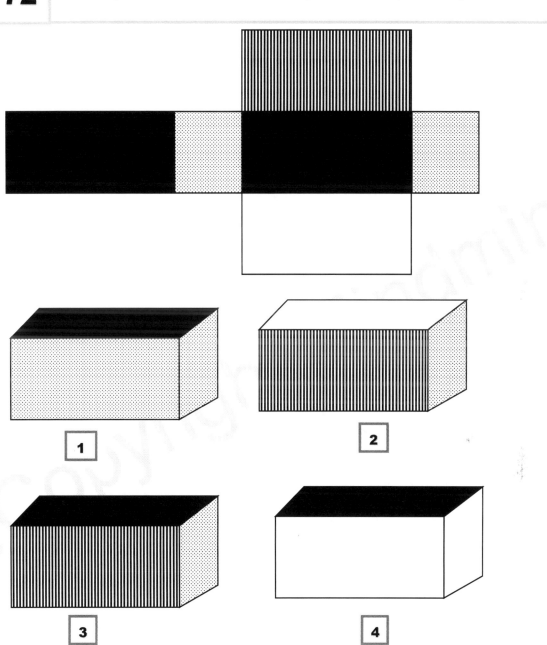

73 Which figure can be assembled using each of the provided pieces?

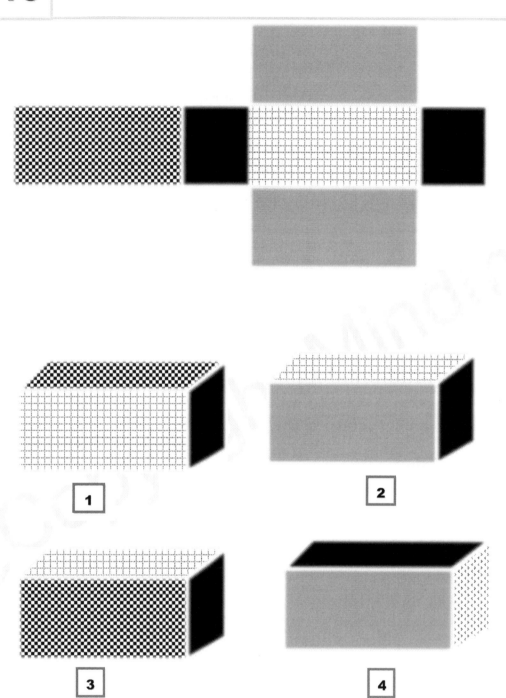

74 Which figure can be assembled using each of the provided pieces?

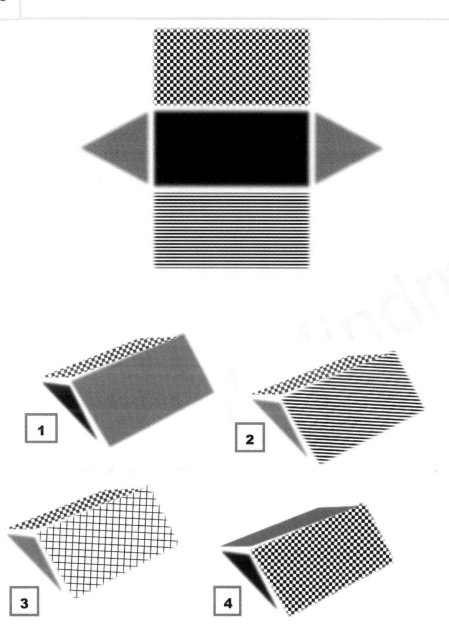

TWO DIMENSIONAL

SPATIAL RELATIONAL THINKING

Turn (Rotation) Fundamental Concepts

C O N C E P T S

TURN CLOCKWISE

  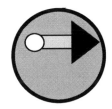

TURN CLOCKWISE

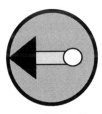  

TURN CLOCKWISE

 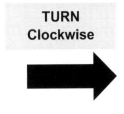 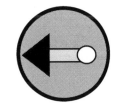

TURN COUNTER-CLOCKWISE

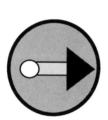 TURN Counter-Clockwise

C
O
N
C
E
P
T
S

TURN COUNTER-CLOCKWISE

 TURN Counter-Clockwise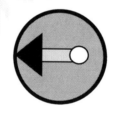

TURN COUNTER-CLOCKWISE

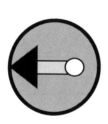  

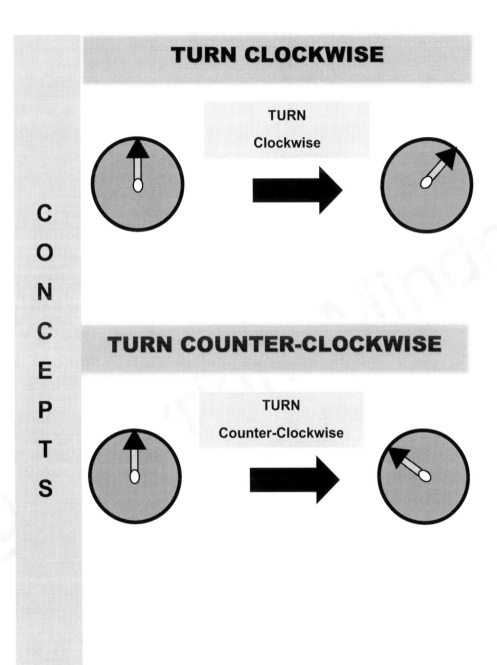

Find the answer that exactly matches the below figure when is turned around or rotated

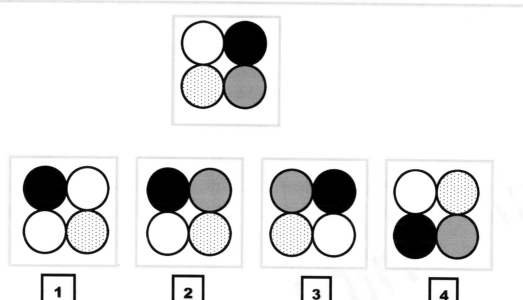

Technique: When a shape is turned (clockwise or counter-clockwise, ORDER of shapes (or color) will remain same.

In the above picture, Order of shapes(colors) clockwise are

1) Black Circle
2) Gray Circle
3) Circle with dots

Answer is: 2

1, 3, 4 are incorrect. Order of colors is incorrect.

| 75 | Find the answer that exactly matches the below figure when is turned around or rotated |

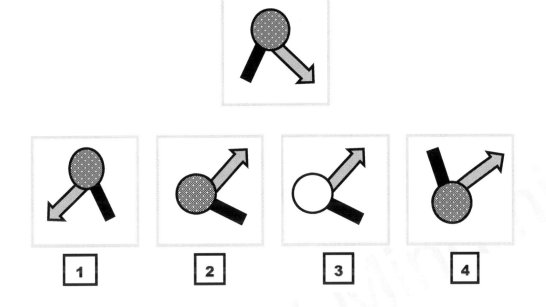

| 76 | Find the answer that exactly matches the below figure when is turned around or rotated |

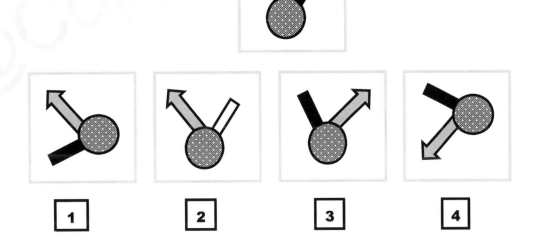

77 Find the answer that exactly matches the below figure when is turned around or rotated

| 1 | 2 | 3 | 4 |

78 Find the answer that exactly matches the below figure when is turned around or rotated

| 1 | 2 | 3 | 4 |

79	Find the answer that exactly matches the below figure when is turned around or rotated

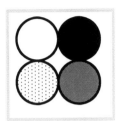

 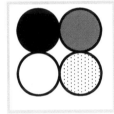 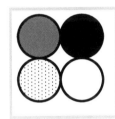 

| 1 | 2 | 3 | 4 |

80	Find the answer that exactly matches the below figure when is turned around or rotated

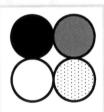

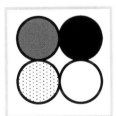   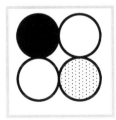

| 1 | 2 | 3 | 4 |

81 Find the answer that exactly matches the below figure when is turned around or rotated

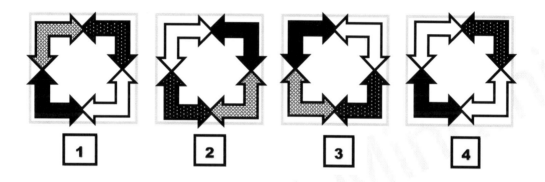

82 Find the answer that exactly matches the below figure when is turned around or rotated

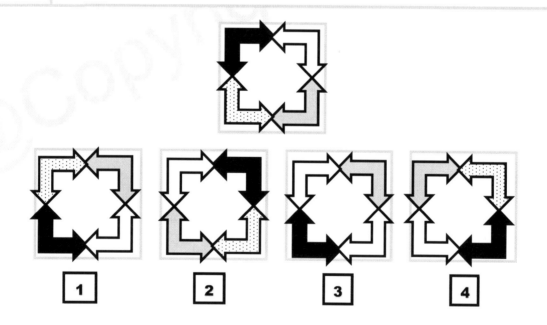

83	Find the answer that exactly matches the below figure when is turned around or rotated

| 1 | 2 | 3 | 4 |

84	Find the answer that exactly matches the below figure when is turned around or rotated

| 1 | 2 | 3 | 4 |

85 Find the answer that exactly matches the below figure when is turned around or rotated

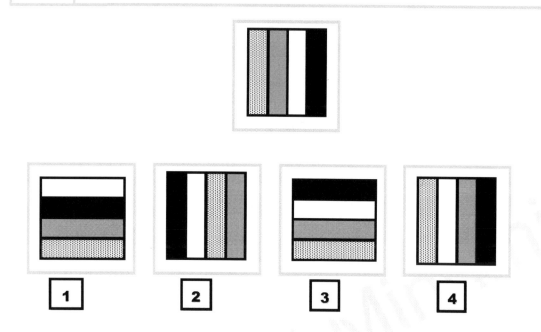

86 Find the answer that exactly matches the below figure when is turned around or rotated

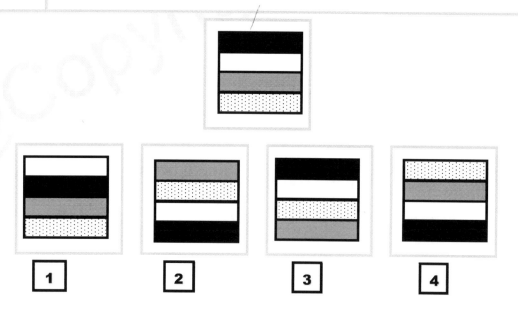

87	Find the answer that exactly matches the below figure when is turned around or rotated

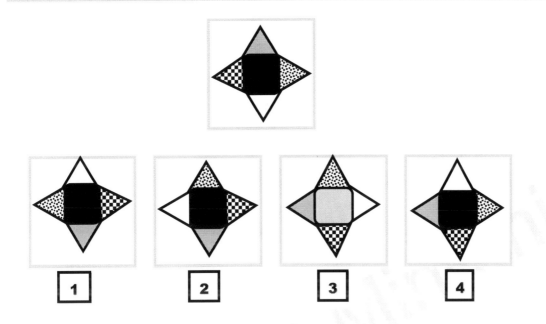

88	Find the answer that exactly matches the below figure when is turned around or rotated

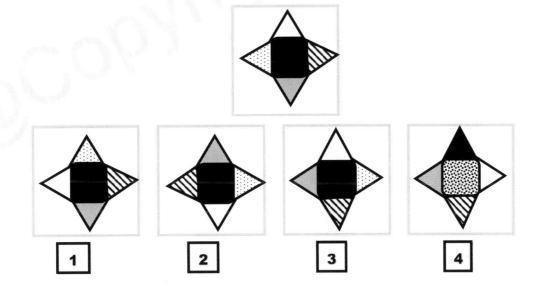

89	Find the answer that exactly matches the below figure when is turned around or rotated

| 1 | 2 | 3 | 4 |

90	Find the answer that exactly matches the below figure when is turned around or rotated

| 1 | 2 | 3 | 4 |

91 Find the answer that exactly matches the below figure when is turned around or rotated

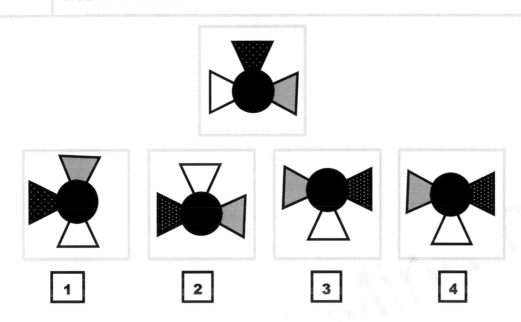

92 Find the answer that exactly matches the below figure when is turned around or rotated

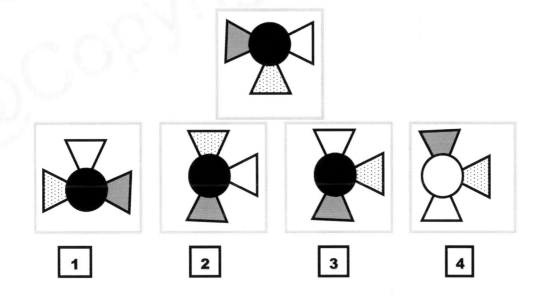

93	Find the answer that exactly matches the below figure when is turned around or rotated

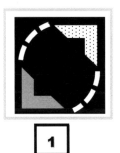  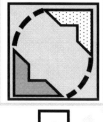 

| 1 | 2 | 3 | 4 |

94	Find the answer that exactly matches the below figure when is turned around or rotated

| 1 | 2 | 3 | 4 |

110

95 Find the answer that exactly matches the below figure when is turned around or rotated

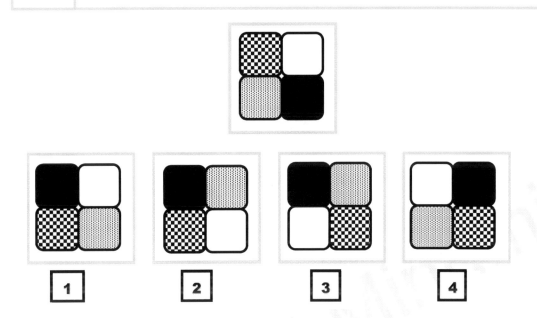

96 Find the answer that exactly matches the below figure when is turned around or rotated

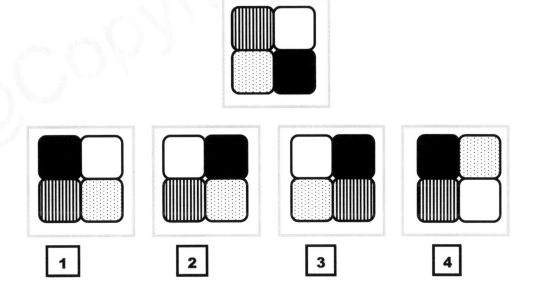

97 Find the answer that exactly matches the below figure when is turned around or rotated

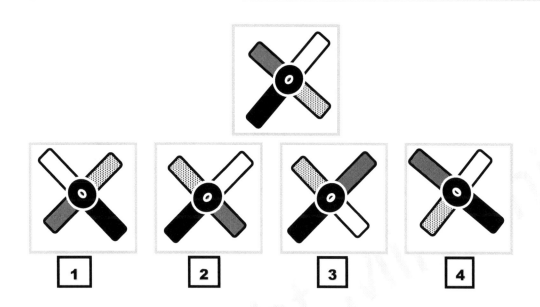

98 Find the answer that exactly matches the below figure when is turned around or rotated

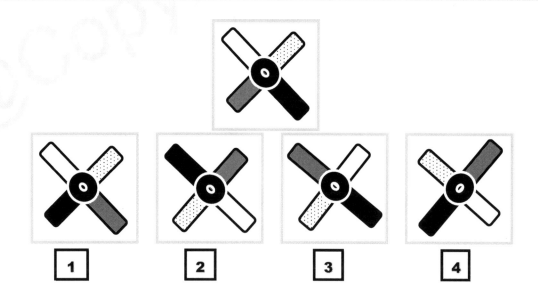

99 Find the answer that exactly matches the below figure when is turned around or rotated

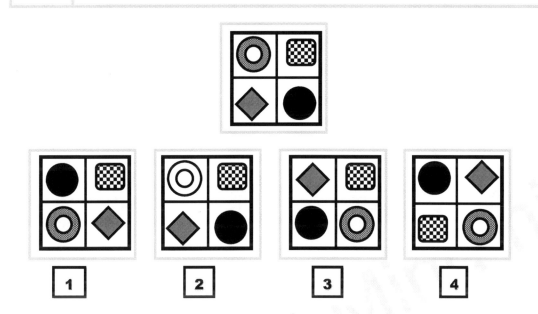

100 Find the answer that exactly matches the below figure when is turned around or rotated

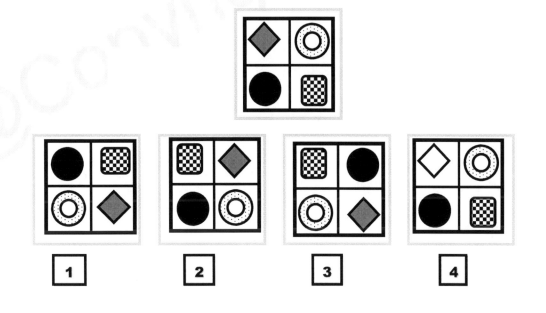

101 Find the answer that exactly matches the below figure when is turned around or rotated

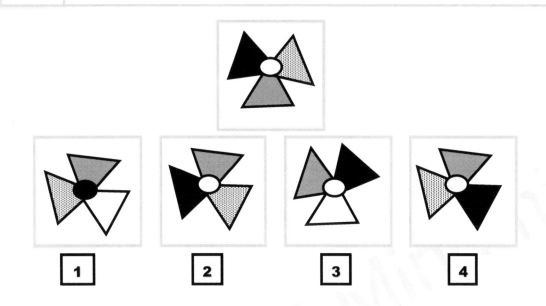

102 Find the answer that exactly matches the below figure when is turned around or rotated

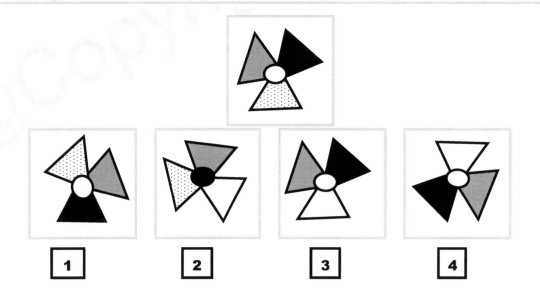

103 Find the answer that exactly matches the below figure when is turned around or rotated

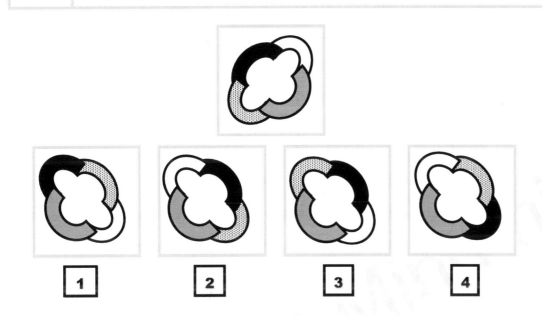

104 Find the answer that exactly matches the below figure when is turned around or rotated

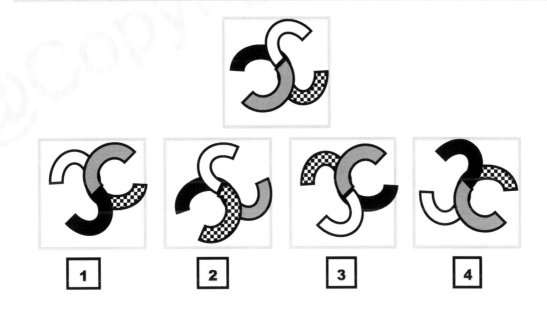

105 Find the answer that exactly matches the below figure when is turned around or rotated

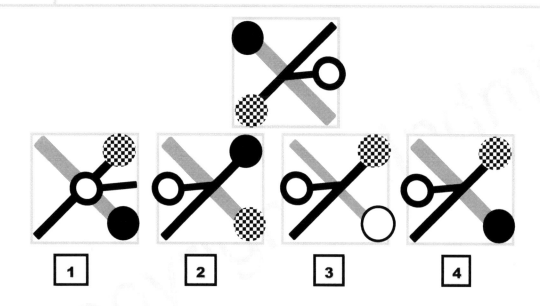

SPATIAL THINKING

ABSTRACT REASONING

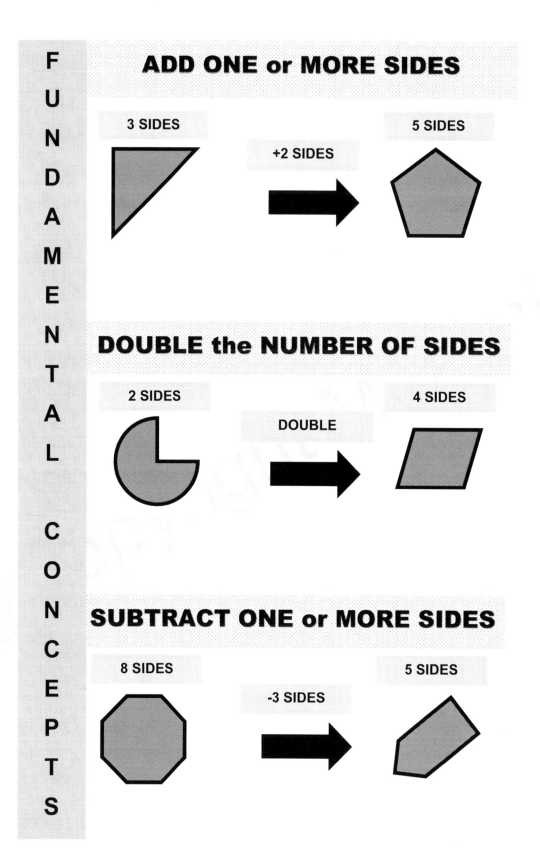

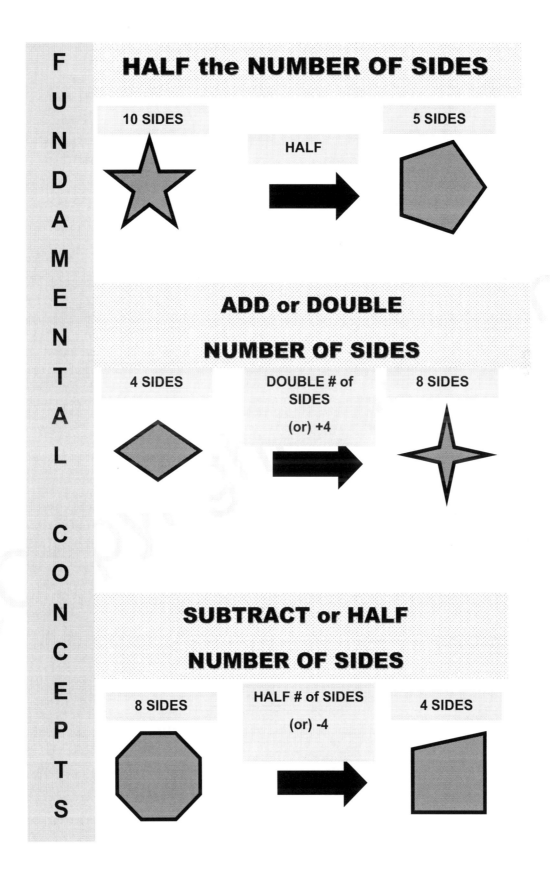

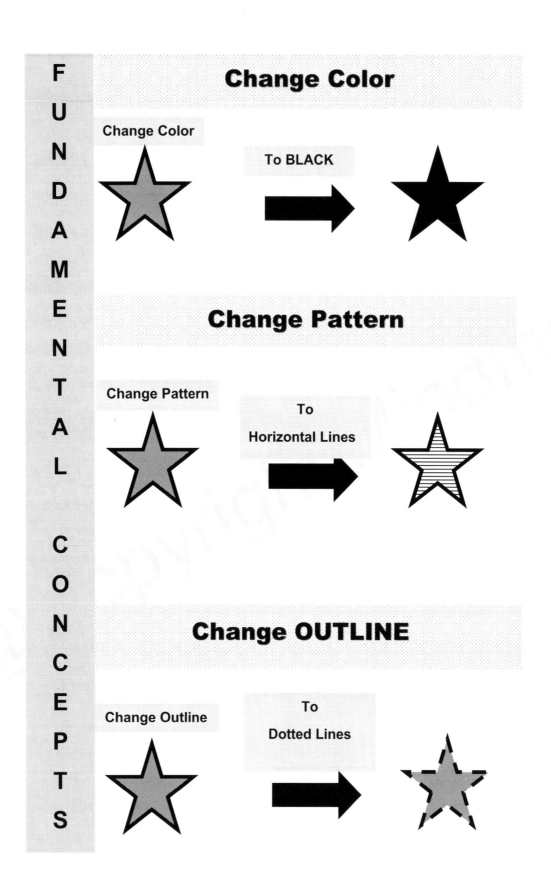

FUNDAMENTAL CONCEPTS

Change Size - Make BIG
(Increase LENGTH & WIDTH)

Change Size – Make SMALL
(Decrease LENGTH & WIDTH)

Change Size
Increase Length (or Base) ONLY

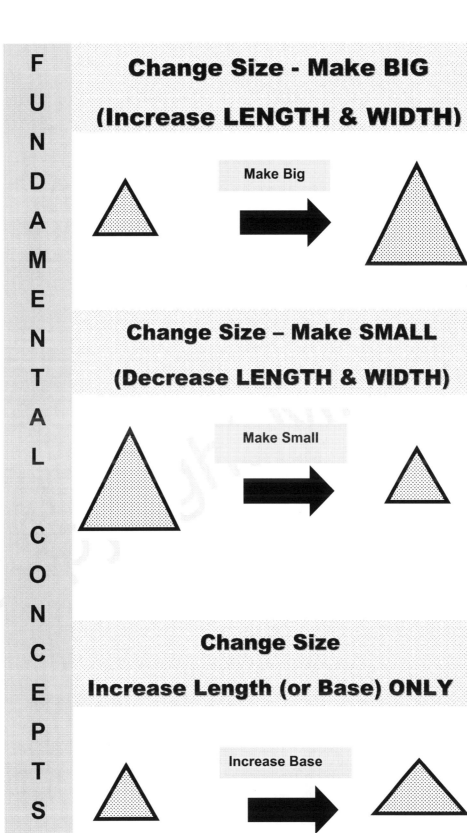

FUNDAMENTAL CONCEPTS

Change Size
Increase HEIGHT ONLY

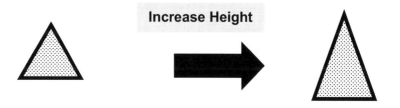

Change Size
Decrease Length (or Base) ONLY

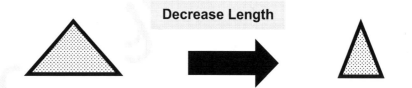

Change Size
Decrease HEIGHT ONLY

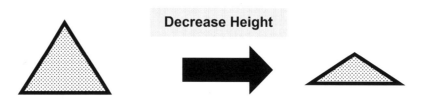

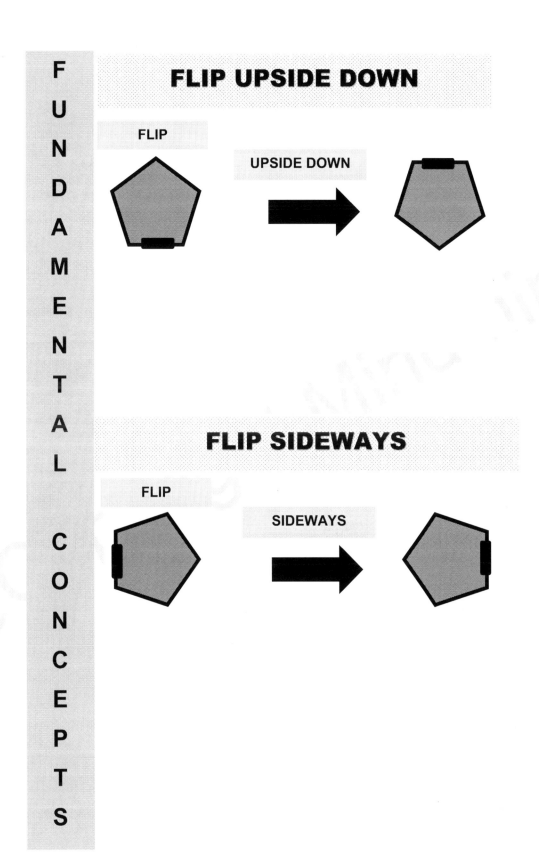

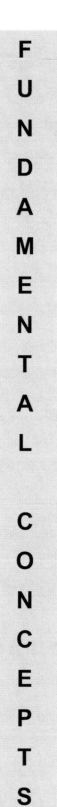

FLIP UPSIDE DOWN

FLIP   **UPSIDE DOWN** ➡

Note: Same shape results when flipped upside down

FLIP SIDEWAYS

FLIP   **SIDEWAYS** ➡

Note: Same shape results when flipped sideways

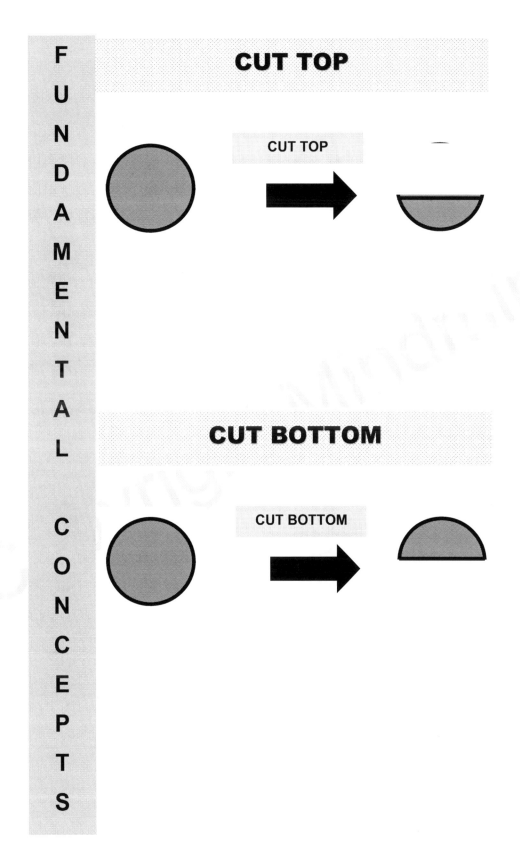

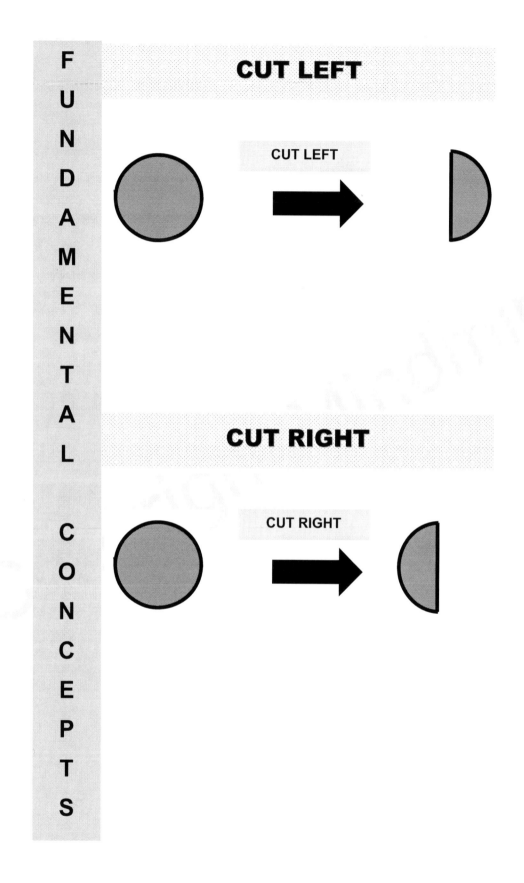

F U N D A M E N T A L   C O N C E P T S

ADD a FIGURE

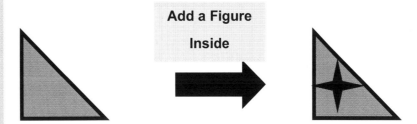

ADD SAME FIGURE

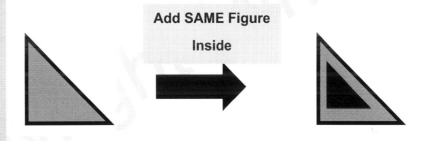

ADD a FIGURE

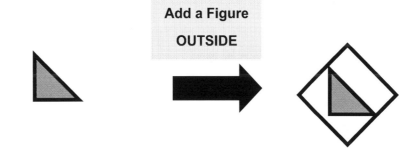

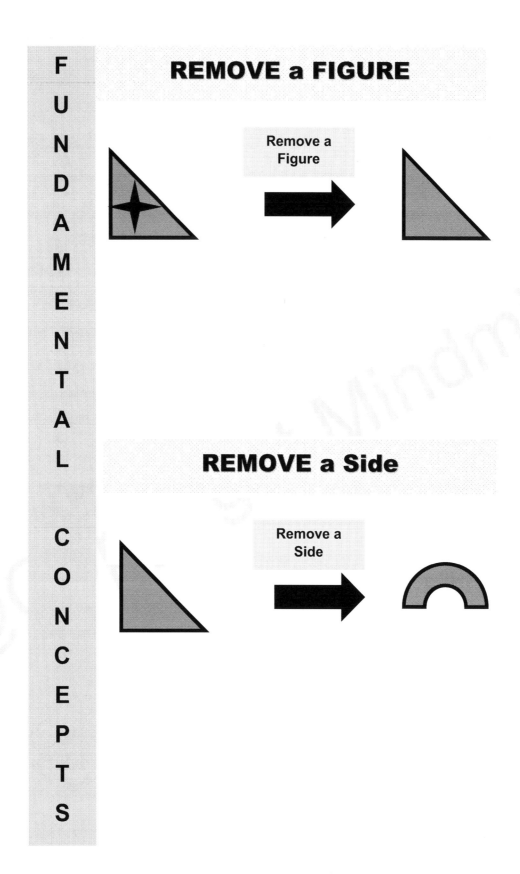

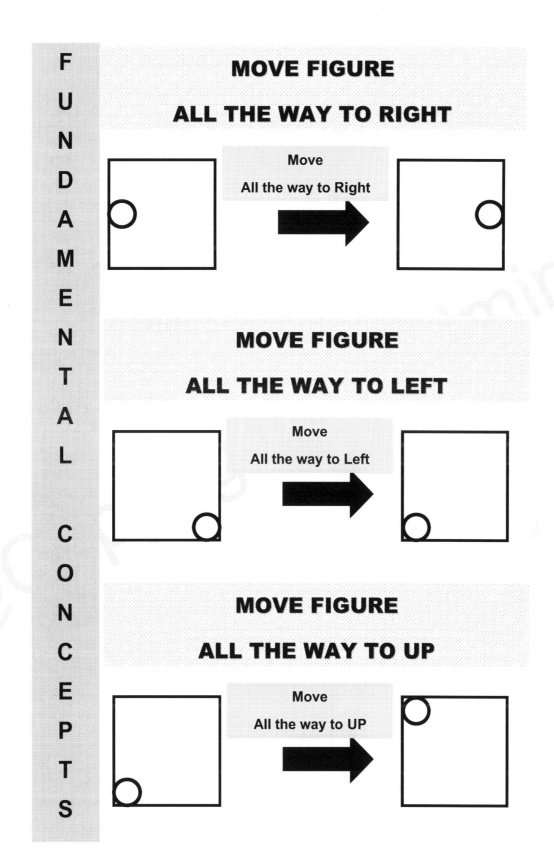

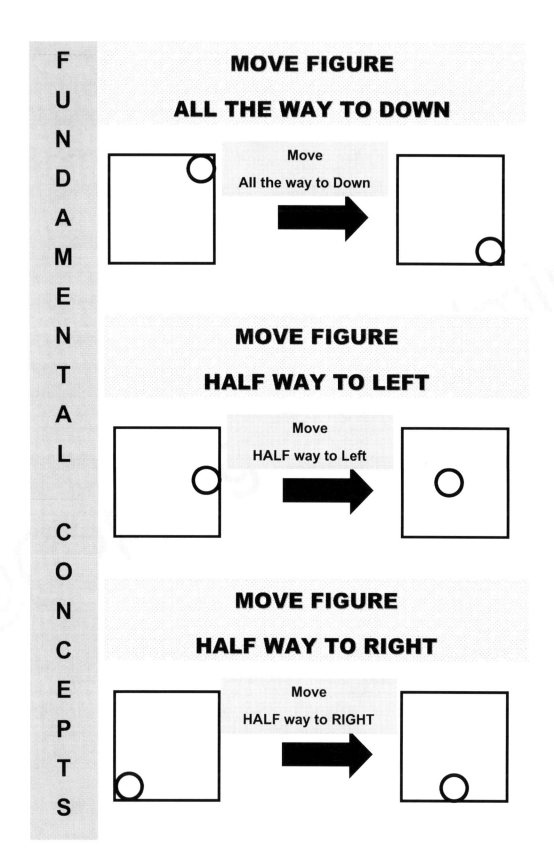

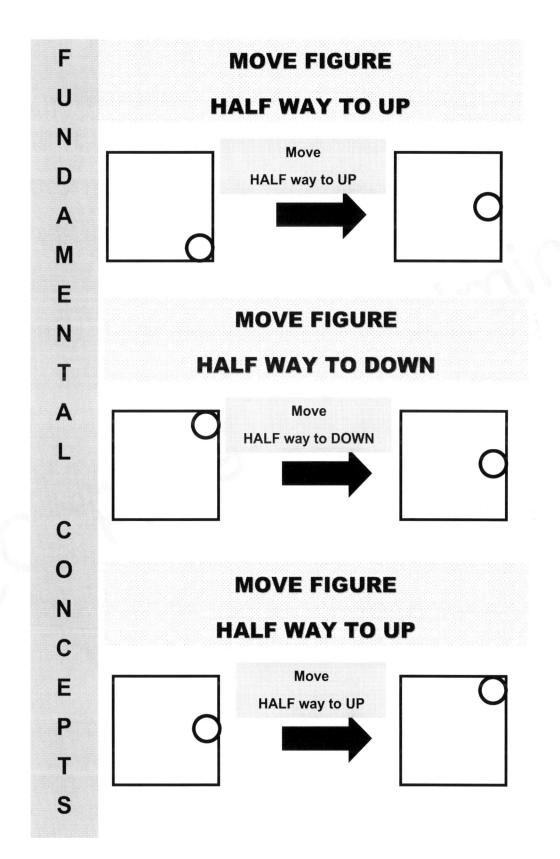

FUNDAMENTAL CONCEPTS

SWAP POSITION
BRING FRONT/SEND BACK

SWAP POSITION
BRING FRONT/SEND BACK

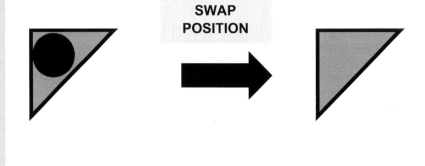

FUNDAMENTAL CONCEPTS

SWAP POSITION
SWAP PLACE

SWAP COLOR

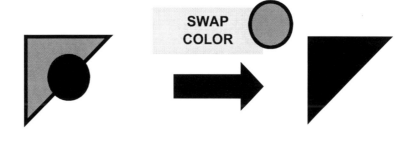

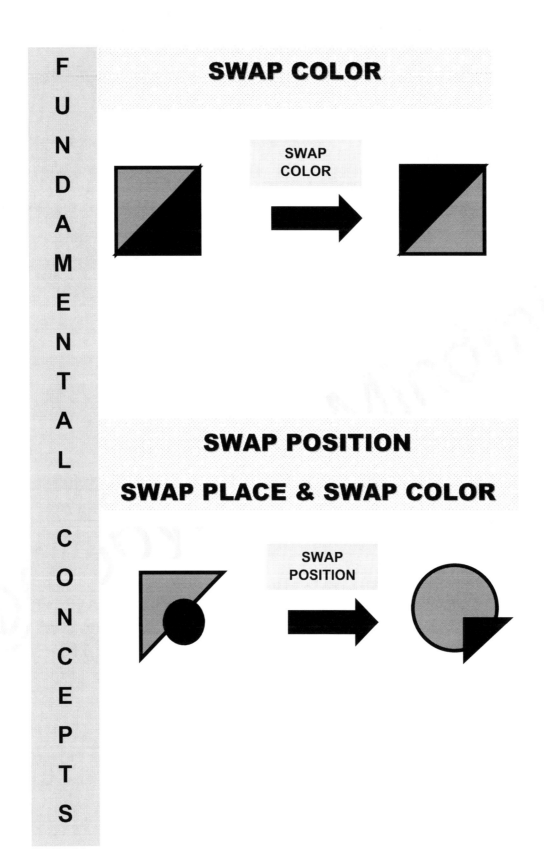

A set of figures are arranged in a pattern below. Find the answer that belongs where question mark is?

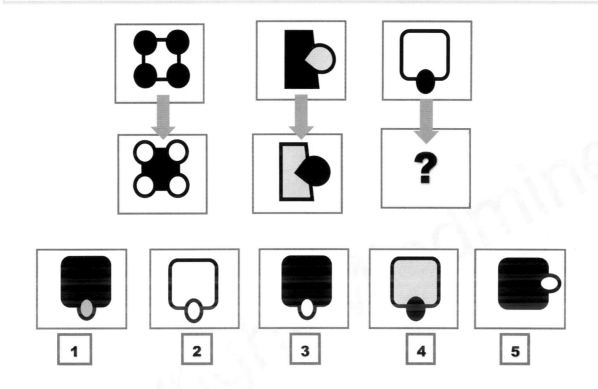

Analogy is "Swap Color"

Answer is "3"

106 A set of figures are arranged in a pattern below. Find the answer that belongs where question mark is?

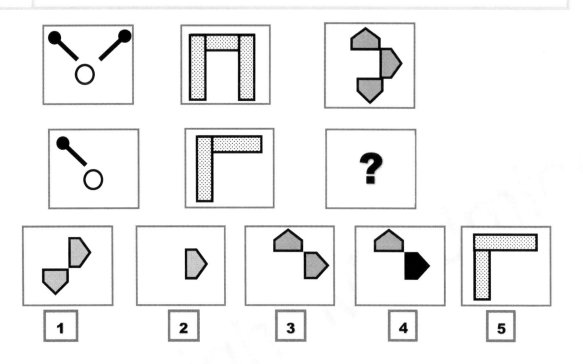

107 A set of figures are arranged in a pattern below. Find the answer that belongs where question mark is?

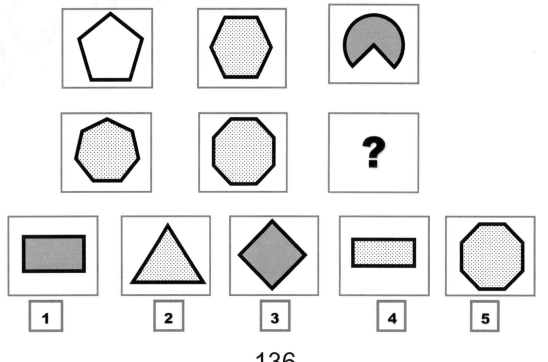

108 A set of figures are arranged in a pattern below. Find the answer that belongs where question mark is?

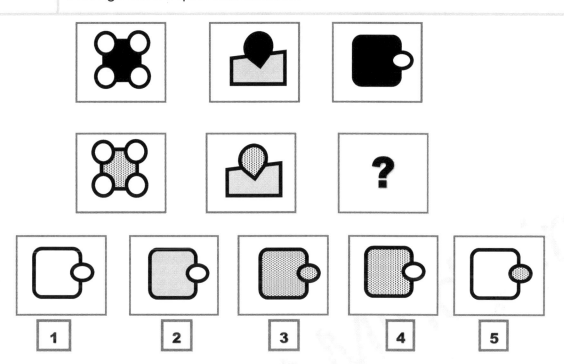

109 A set of figures are arranged in a pattern below. Find the answer that belongs where question mark is?

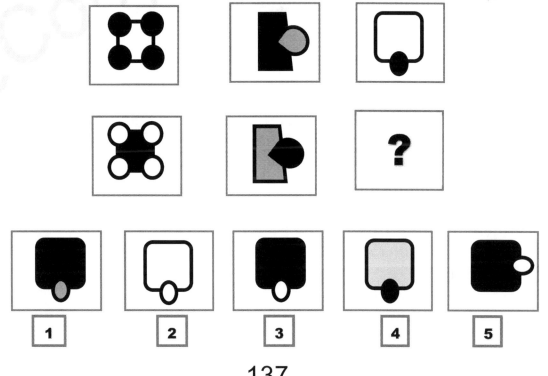

110 A set of figures are arranged in a pattern below. Find the answer that belongs where question mark is?

111 A set of figures are arranged in a pattern below. Find the answer that belongs where question mark is?

112 A set of figures are arranged in a pattern below. Find the answer that belongs where question mark is?

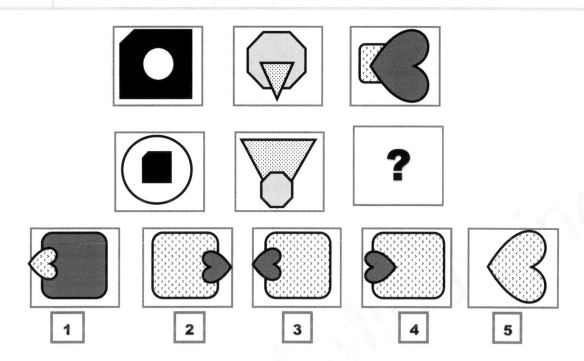

113 A set of figures are arranged in a pattern below. Find the answer that belongs where question mark is?

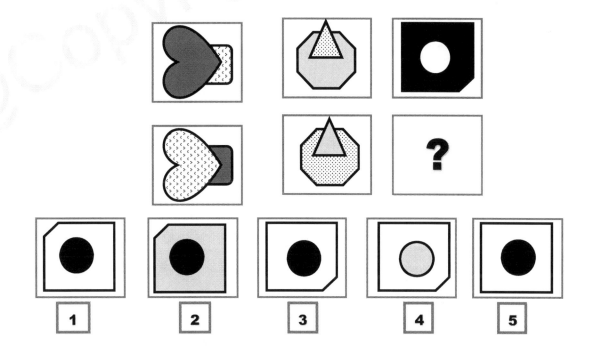

114 A set of figures are arranged in a pattern below. Find the answer that belongs where question mark is?

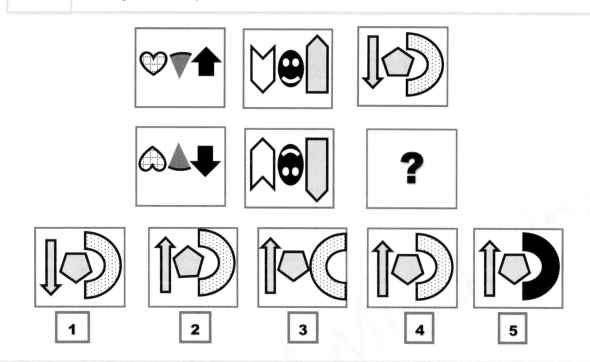

115 A set of figures are arranged in a pattern below. Find the answer that belongs where question mark is?

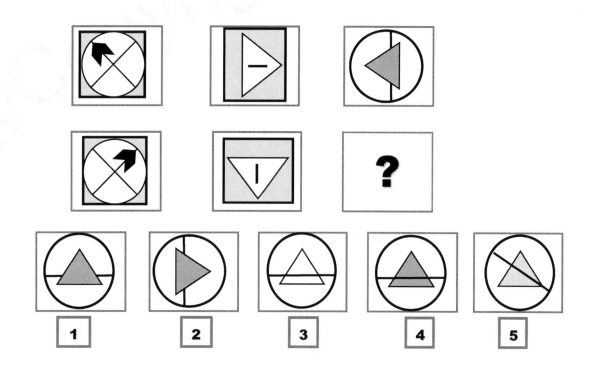

116 A set of figures are arranged in a pattern below. Find the answer that belongs where question mark is?

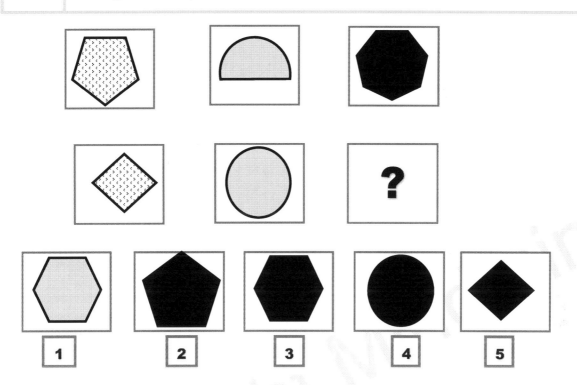

117 A set of figures are arranged in a pattern below. Find the answer that belongs where question mark is?

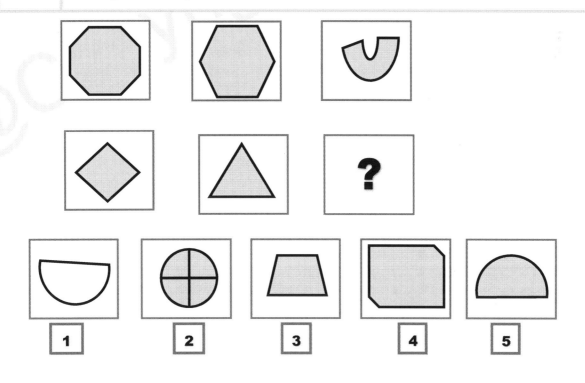

118 A set of figures are arranged in a pattern below. Find the answer that belongs where question mark is?

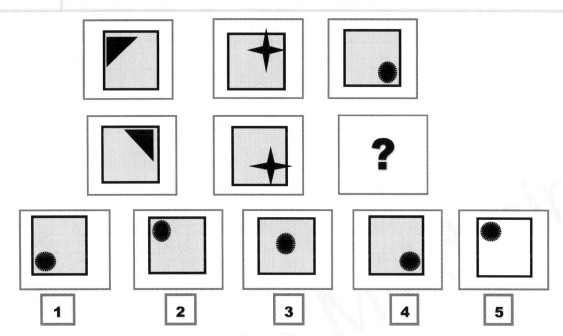

119 A set of figures are arranged in a pattern below. Find the answer that belongs where question mark is?

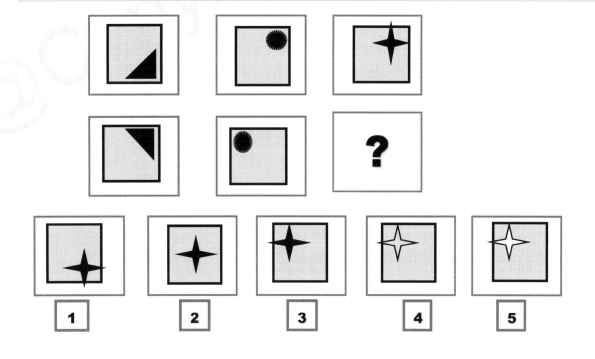

120 A set of figures are arranged in a pattern below. Find the answer that belongs where question mark is?

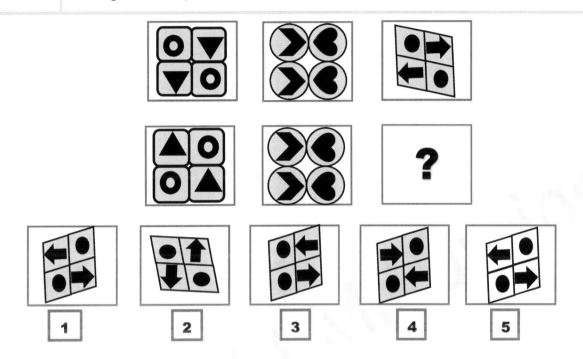

121 A set of figures are arranged in a pattern below. Find the answer that belongs where question mark is?

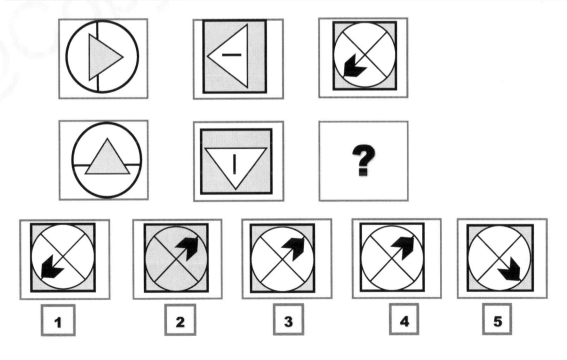

122 A set of figures are arranged in a pattern below. Find the answer that belongs where question mark is?

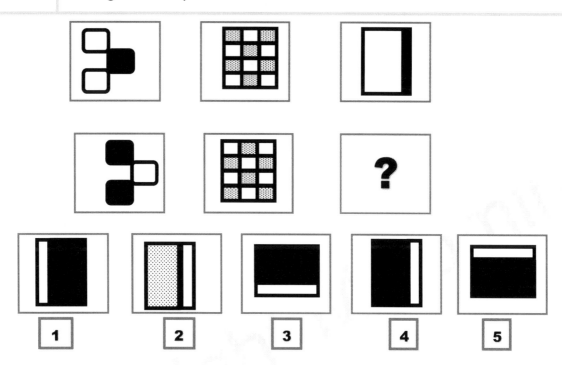

123 A set of figures are arranged in a pattern below. Find the answer that belongs where question mark is?

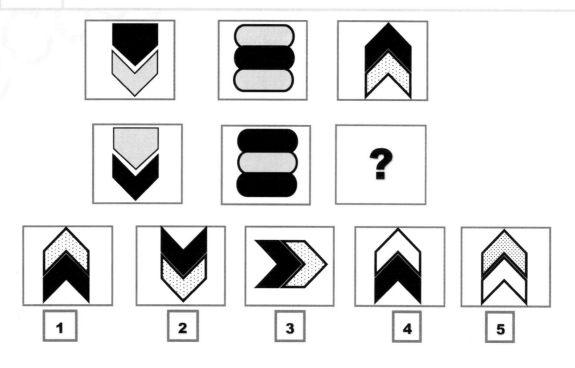

124 A set of figures are arranged in a pattern below. Find the answer that belongs where question mark is?

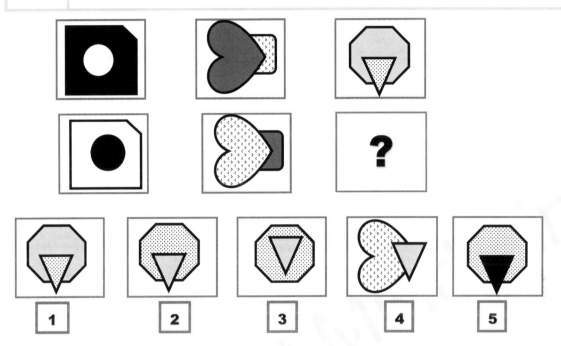

125 A set of figures are arranged in a pattern below. Find the answer that belongs where question mark is?

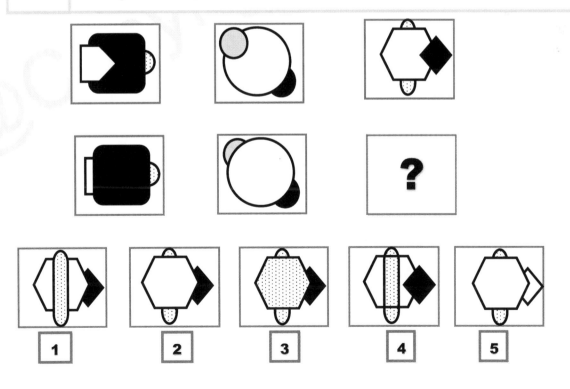

126 A set of figures are arranged in a pattern below. Find the answer that belongs where question mark is?

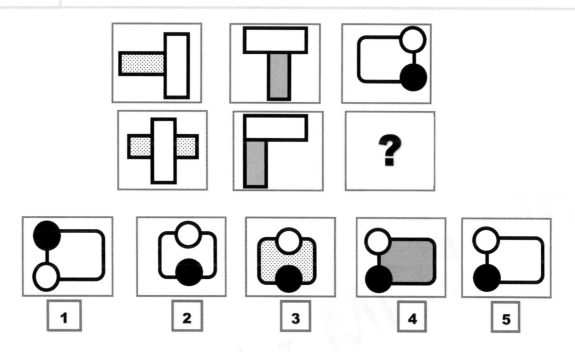

127 A set of figures are arranged in a pattern below. Find the answer that belongs where question mark is?

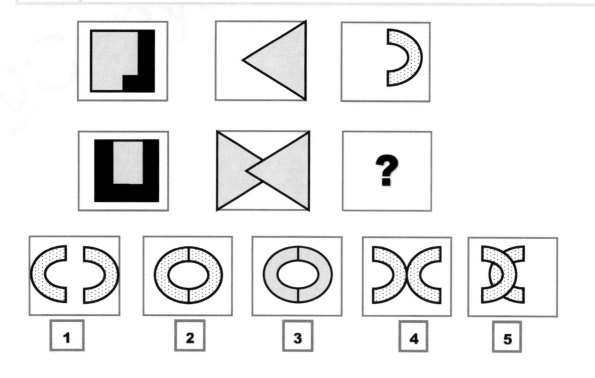

128 A set of figures are arranged in a pattern below. Find the answer that belongs where question mark is?

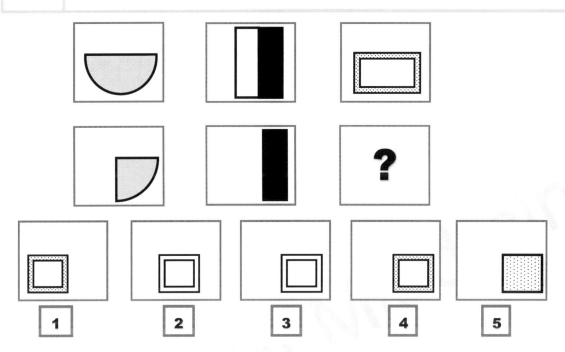

129 A set of figures are arranged in a pattern below. Find the answer that belongs where question mark is?

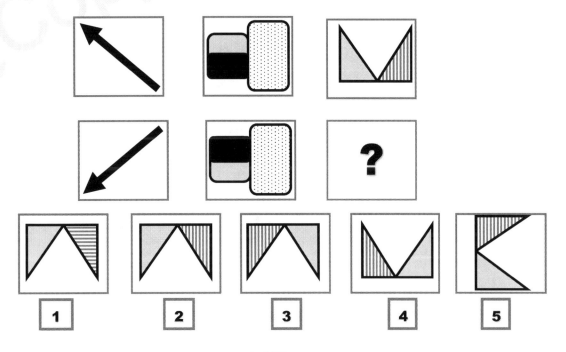

130 A set of figures are arranged in a pattern below. Find the answer that belongs where question mark is?

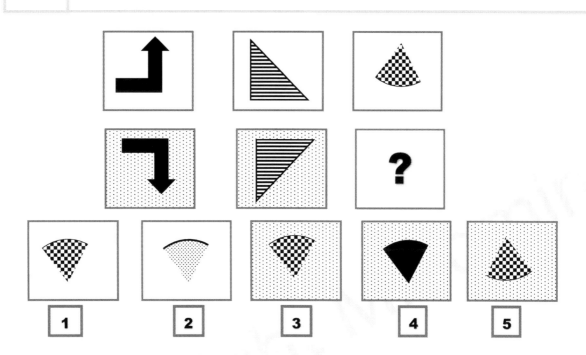

131 A set of figures are arranged in a pattern below. Find the answer that belongs where question mark is?

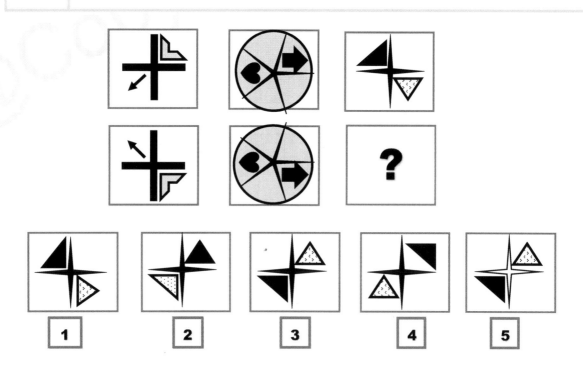

132 A set of figures are arranged in a pattern below. Find the answer that belongs where question mark is?

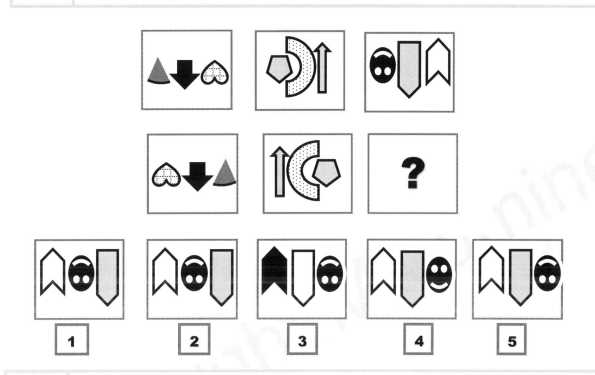

133 A set of figures are arranged in a pattern below. Find the answer that belongs where question mark is?

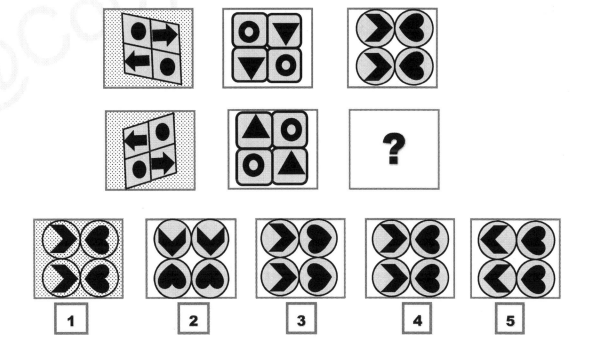

134 A set of figures are arranged in a pattern below. Find the answer that belongs where question mark is?

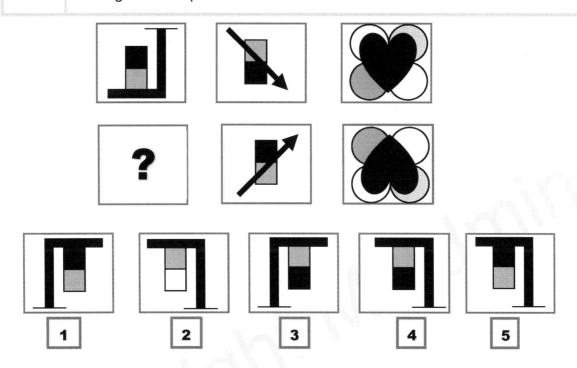

135 A set of figures are arranged in a pattern below. Find the answer that belongs where question mark is?

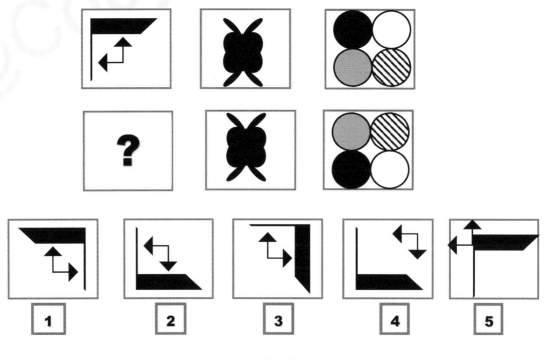

SPATIAL ABILITY

RELATIONAL THINKING

| 136 | Mike came out from the corporate buildings and wanted to go to the ABC office building. He walked few minutes on Murphy road, turned to 15th street, and started walking towards the ABC office building. What direction is Mike going? |

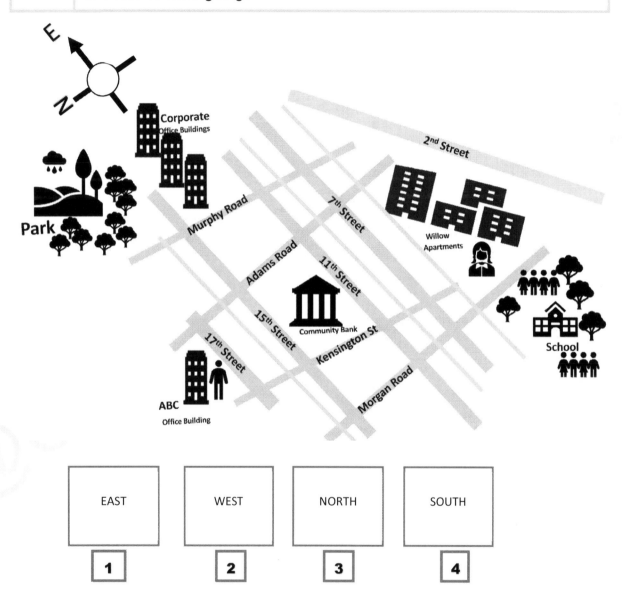

EAST	WEST	NORTH	SOUTH
1	2	3	4

137 Mary works at a school. She walked few minutes on Morgan road, turned right, walked few minutes, then turned left onto Kensington St. She walked for another 10 minutes and turned right onto 15th street. What direction is Mary facing?

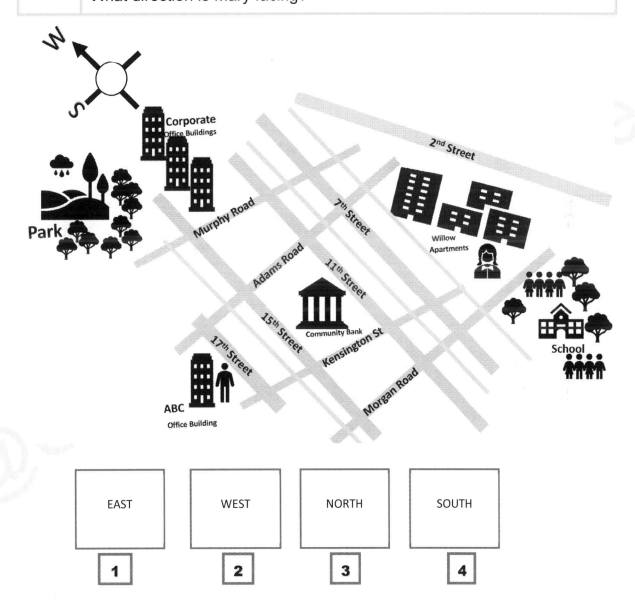

EAST	WEST	NORTH	SOUTH
1	2	3	4

| 138 | John came out of the ABC office building and started walking south. William came out of Corporate office building and started walking west. After few minutes, he turned left. Both John and William are going to their homes located at Willow apartments. On which road are they both likely to meet each other? |

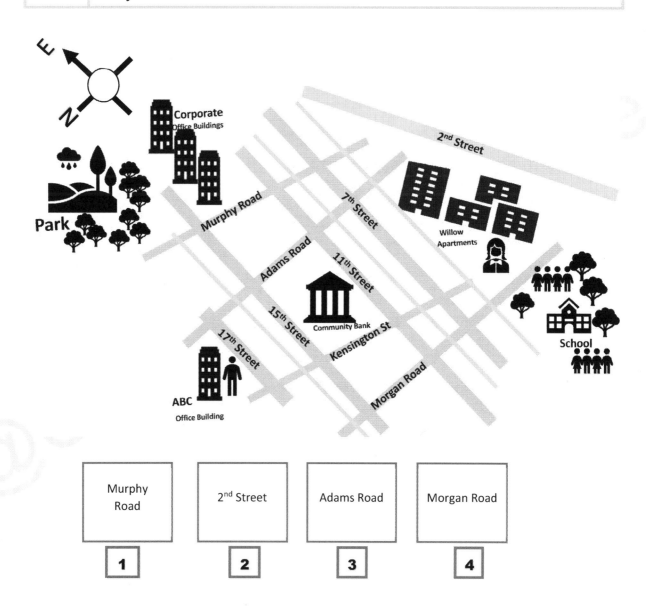

Murphy Road	2nd Street	Adams Road	Morgan Road
1	2	3	4

139 Jennifer comes out of her apartment and walks north on Kensington St, turns right and walks East, turns left onto Adams Road, turns right onto 15th street, and turns left onto Murphy Road. Where is she now?

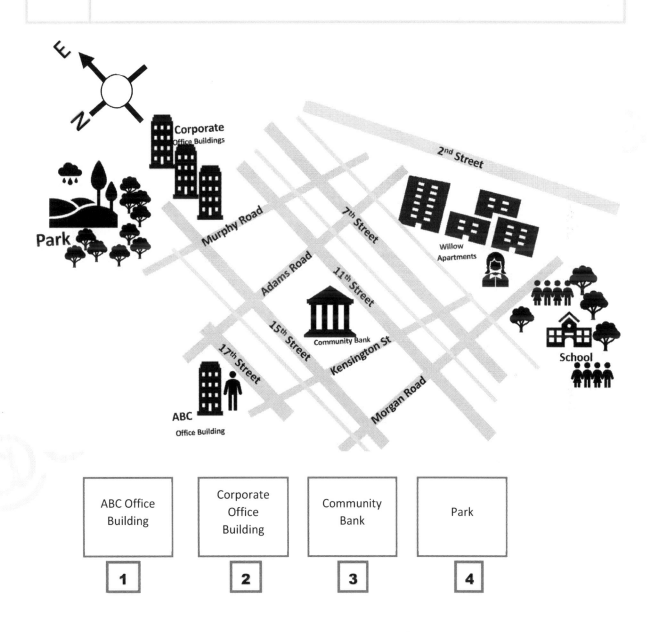

ABC Office Building	Corporate Office Building	Community Bank	Park
1	2	3	4

140 Philips is on 11th street and is walking east. What building would he see next to him?

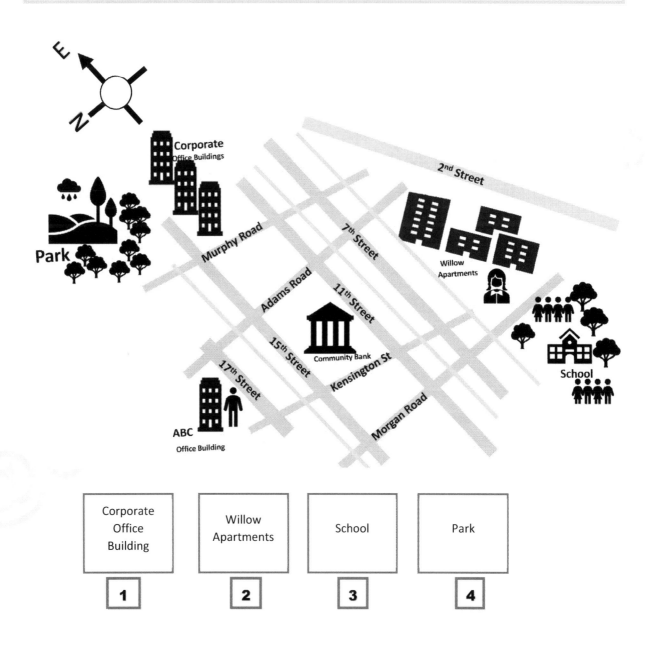

Corporate Office Building	Willow Apartments	School	Park
1	2	3	4

FULL LENGTH PRACTICE TEST

QUESTION #	ANSWER
1	5
2	3
3	4
4	4
5	1
6	3
7	2
8	2
9	2
10	2
11	1
12	3
13	1
14	2
15	1
16	4
17	5
18	1
19	4
20	5

ANSWERS

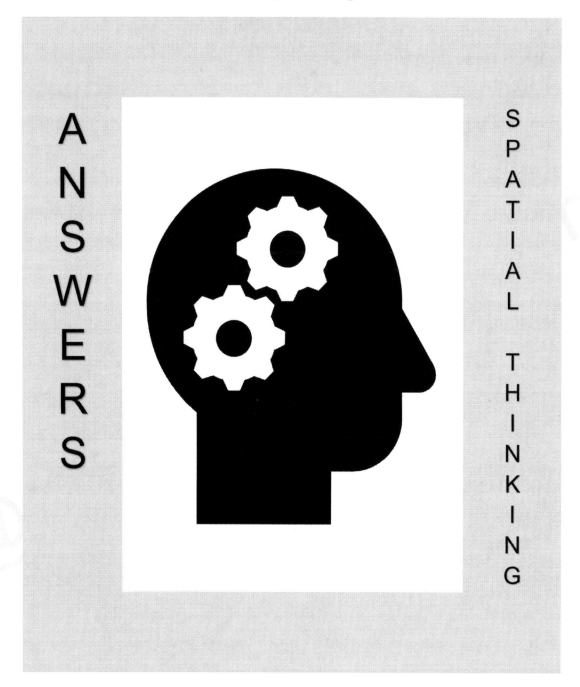

ANSWERS

QUESTION #	ANSWER	Reasoning
1	4	
2	3	
3	2	
4	1	
5	3	
6	3	
7	3	
8	3	
9	5	
10	2	
11	3	
12	1	
13	4	
14	5	
15	5	
16	2	
17	3	
18	4	
19	2	
20	3	
21	4	
22	5	
23	5	
24	4	
25	3	
26	3	
27	4	
28	3	

ANSWERS

QUESTION #	ANSWER	Reasoning
29	4	
30	5	
31	3	
32	1	
33	2	
34	2	
35	3	
36	5	
37	4	
38	5	
39	5	
40	5	
41	5	**41** A 3-Dimesional Cube is shown below with three different views. Which face is across "A"? 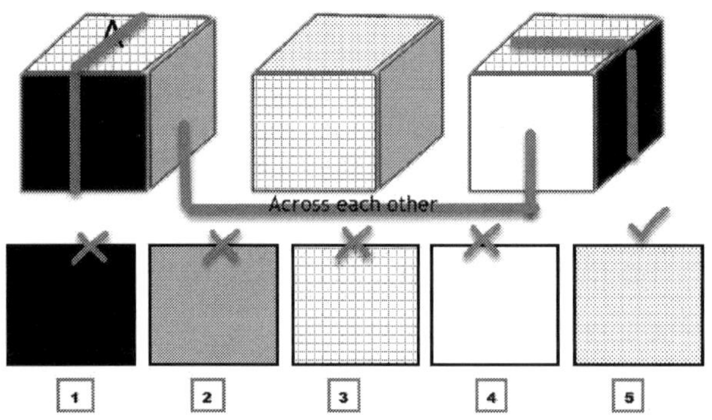 Across each other "A" share faces with 1,2,4. 2nd view comes when 1st view is rotated.

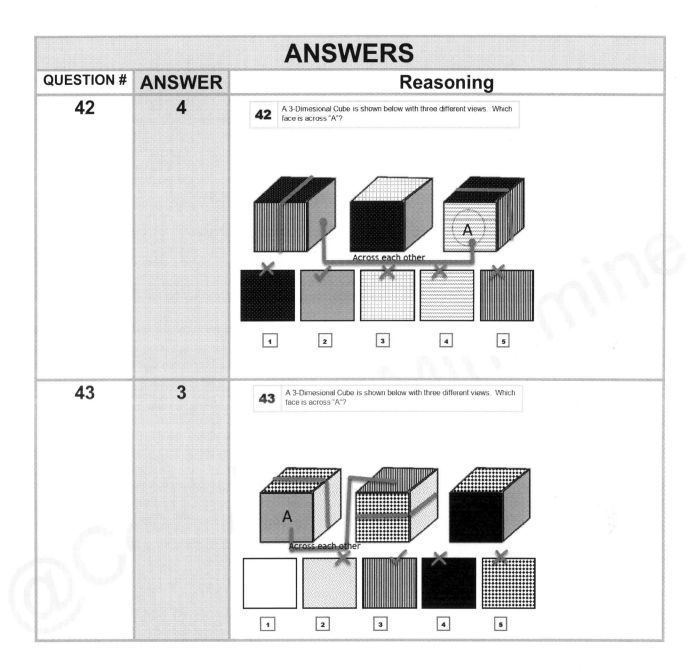

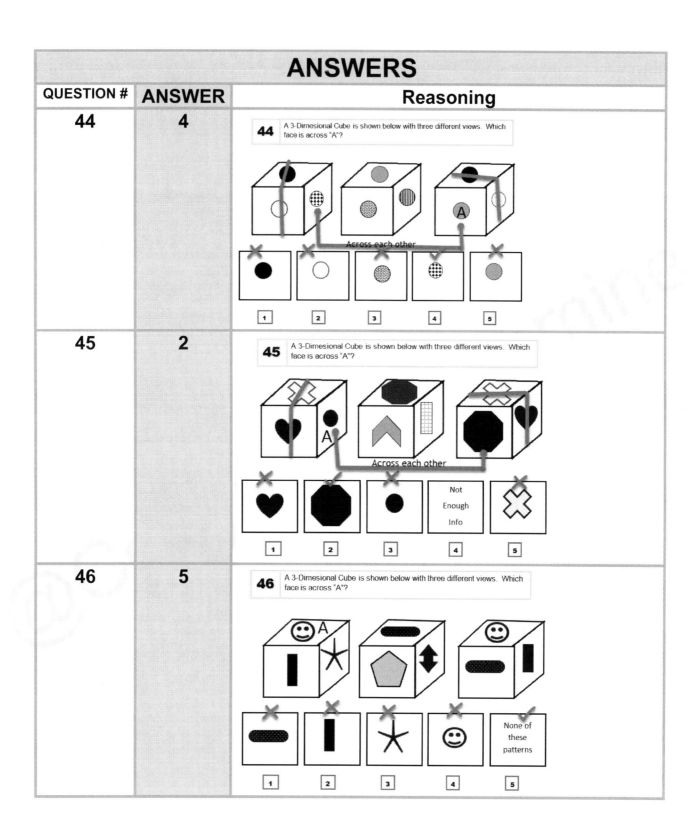

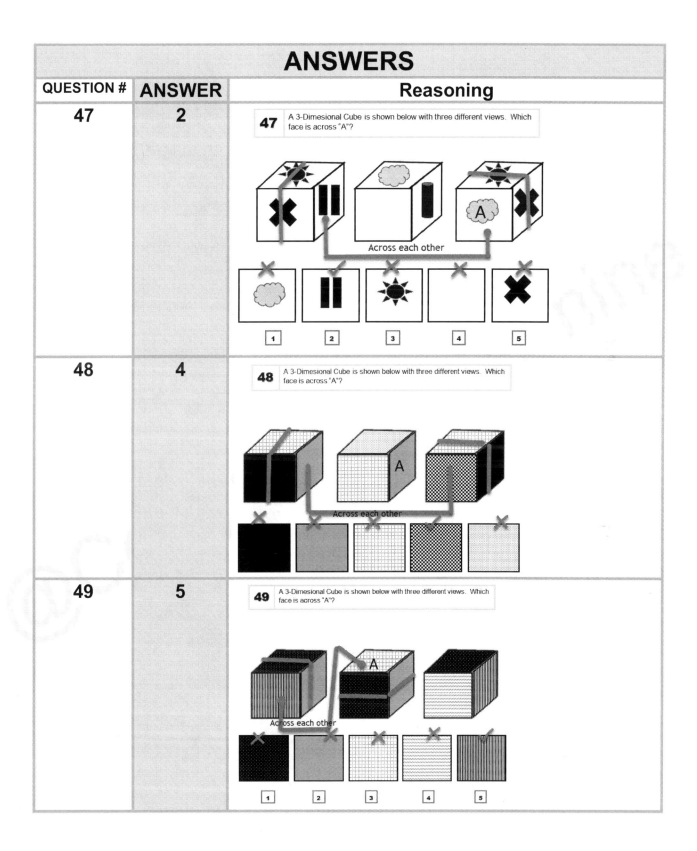

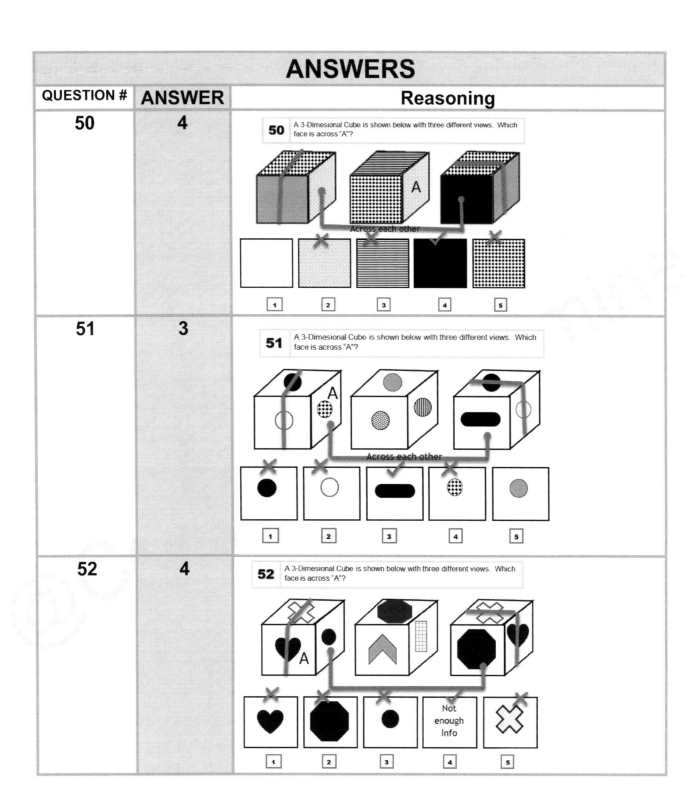

ANSWERS

QUESTION #	ANSWER	Reasoning
53	5	
54	4	
55	4	

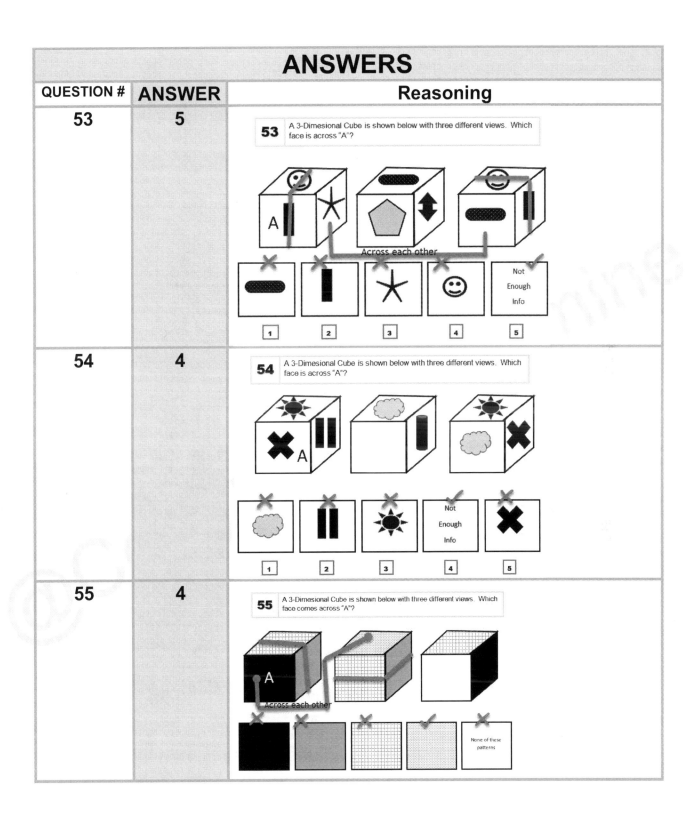

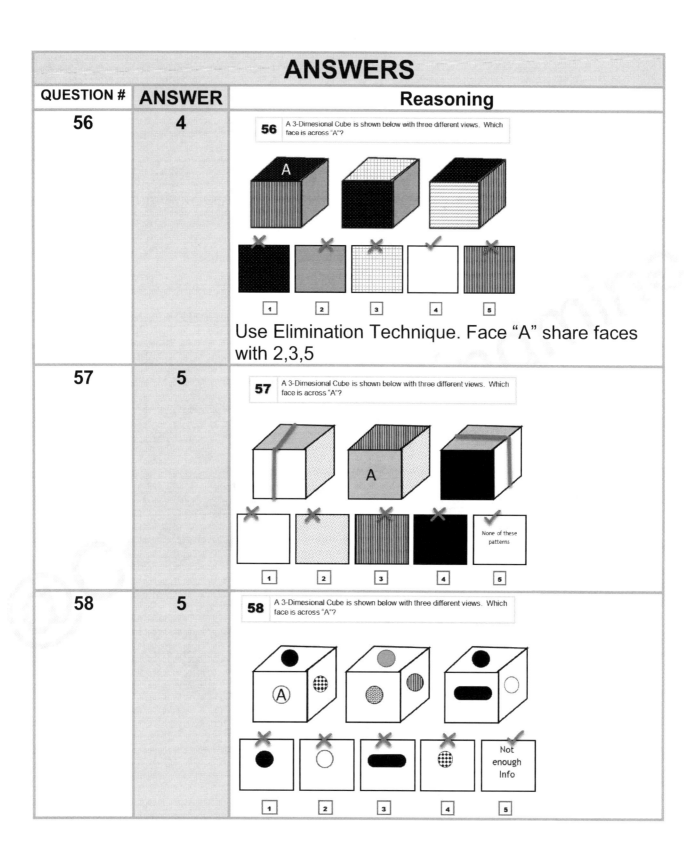

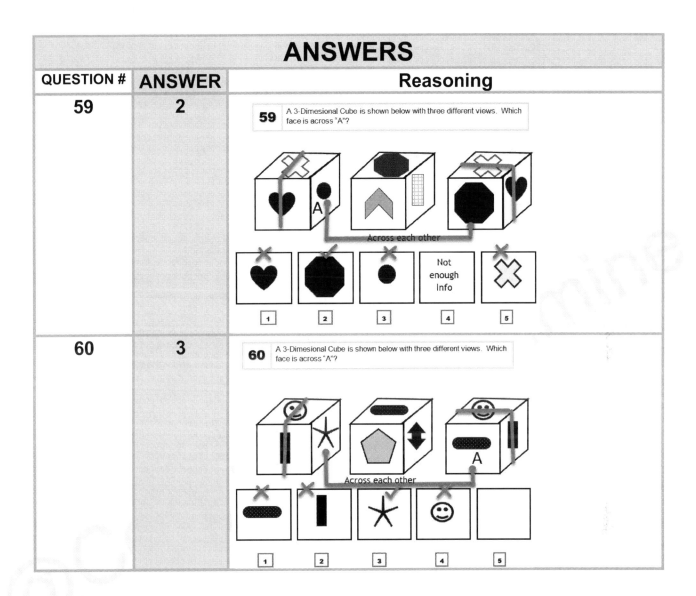

ANSWERS

QUESTION #	ANSWER	Reasoning
61	1	
62	3	

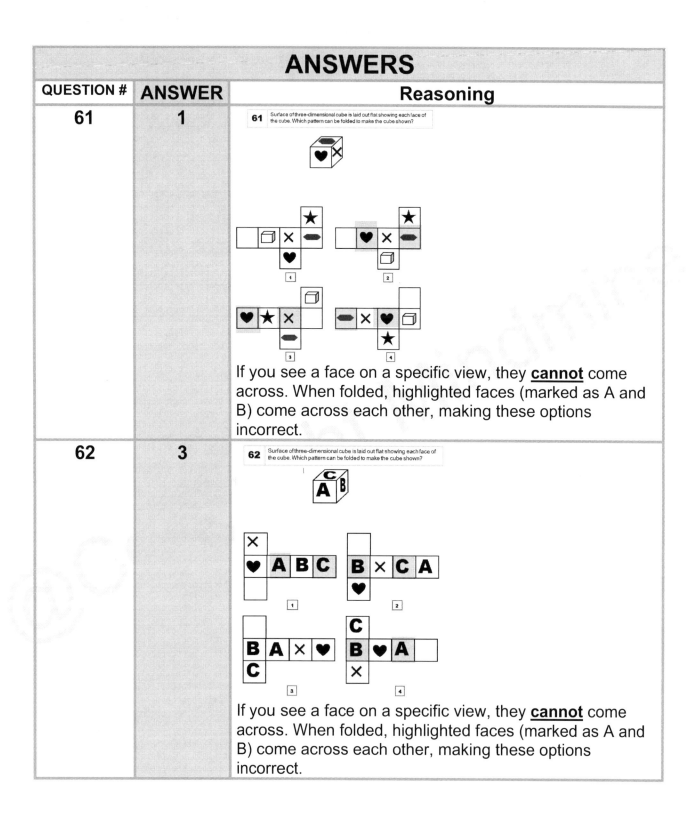

If you see a face on a specific view, they **cannot** come across. When folded, highlighted faces (marked as A and B) come across each other, making these options incorrect.

If you see a face on a specific view, they **cannot** come across. When folded, highlighted faces (marked as A and B) come across each other, making these options incorrect.

ANSWERS

QUESTION #	ANSWER	Reasoning
63	1	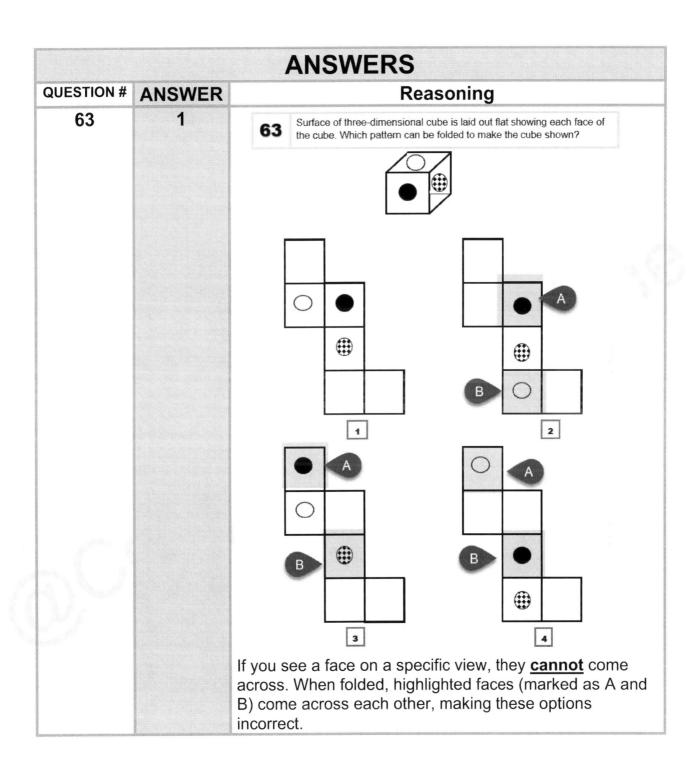 If you see a face on a specific view, they **cannot** come across. When folded, highlighted faces (marked as A and B) come across each other, making these options incorrect.

ANSWERS

QUESTION #	ANSWER	Reasoning
64	2	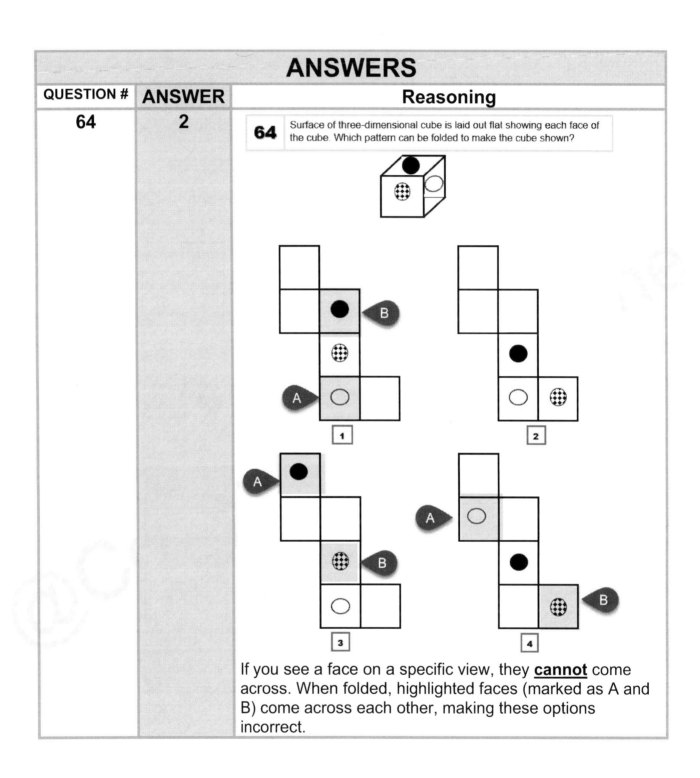 If you see a face on a specific view, they **cannot** come across. When folded, highlighted faces (marked as A and B) come across each other, making these options incorrect.

ANSWERS

QUESTION #	ANSWER	Reasoning
65	4	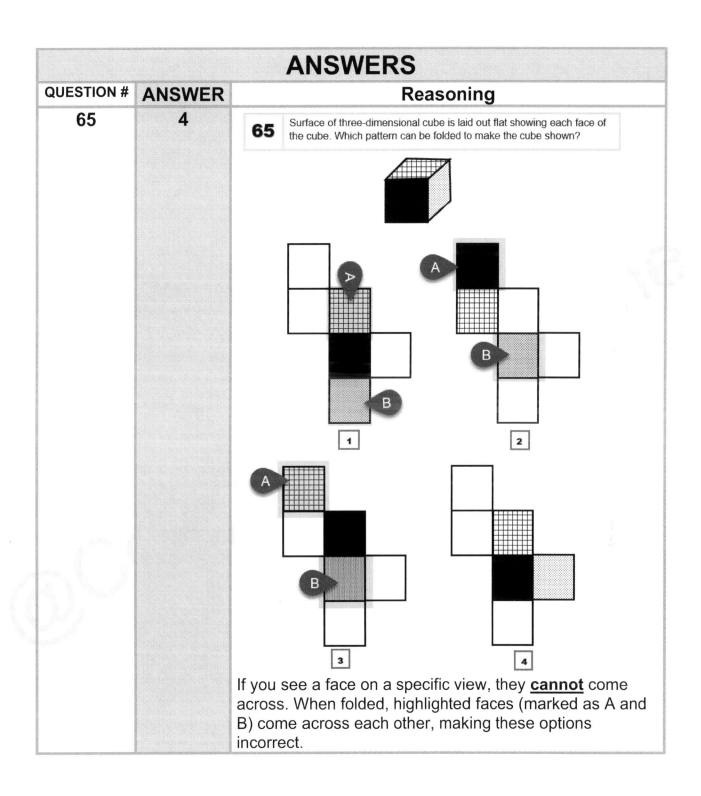 65 Surface of three-dimensional cube is laid out flat showing each face of the cube. Which pattern can be folded to make the cube shown? If you see a face on a specific view, they **cannot** come across. When folded, highlighted faces (marked as A and B) come across each other, making these options incorrect.

ANSWERS

QUESTION #	ANSWER	Reasoning
66	3	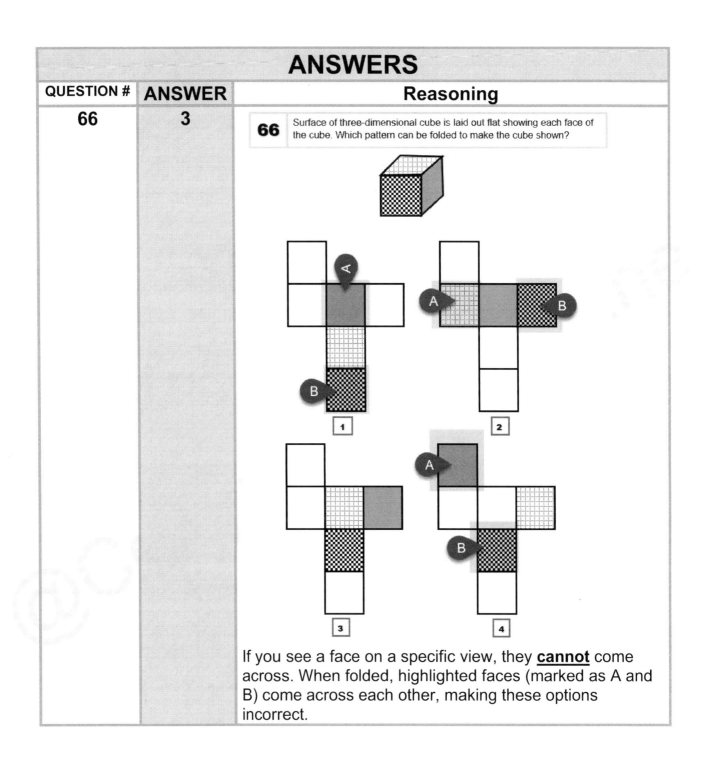

66 Surface of three-dimensional cube is laid out flat showing each face of the cube. Which pattern can be folded to make the cube shown?

If you see a face on a specific view, they **cannot** come across. When folded, highlighted faces (marked as A and B) come across each other, making these options incorrect.

ANSWERS

QUESTION #	ANSWER	Reasoning
67	3	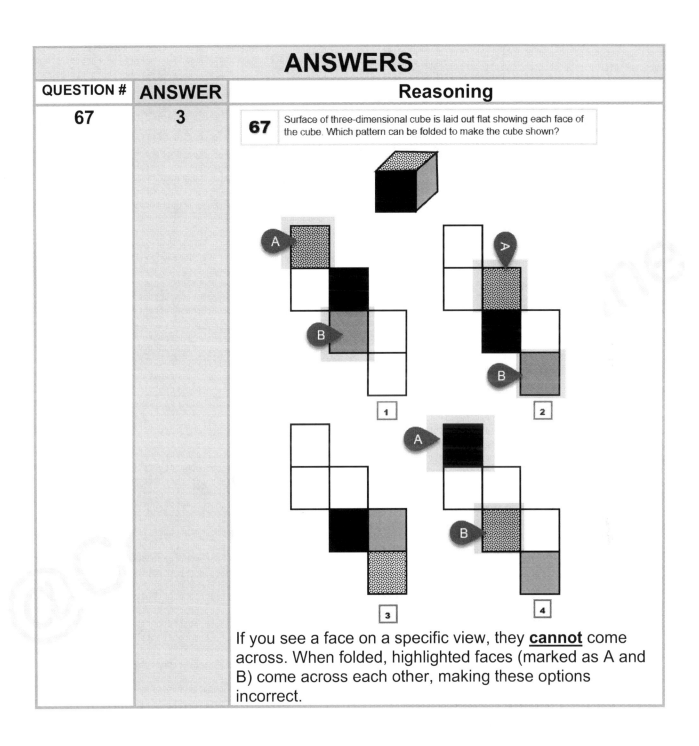 67 Surface of three-dimensional cube is laid out flat showing each face of the cube. Which pattern can be folded to make the cube shown? If you see a face on a specific view, they **cannot** come across. When folded, highlighted faces (marked as A and B) come across each other, making these options incorrect.

ANSWERS

QUESTION #	ANSWER	Reasoning
68	4	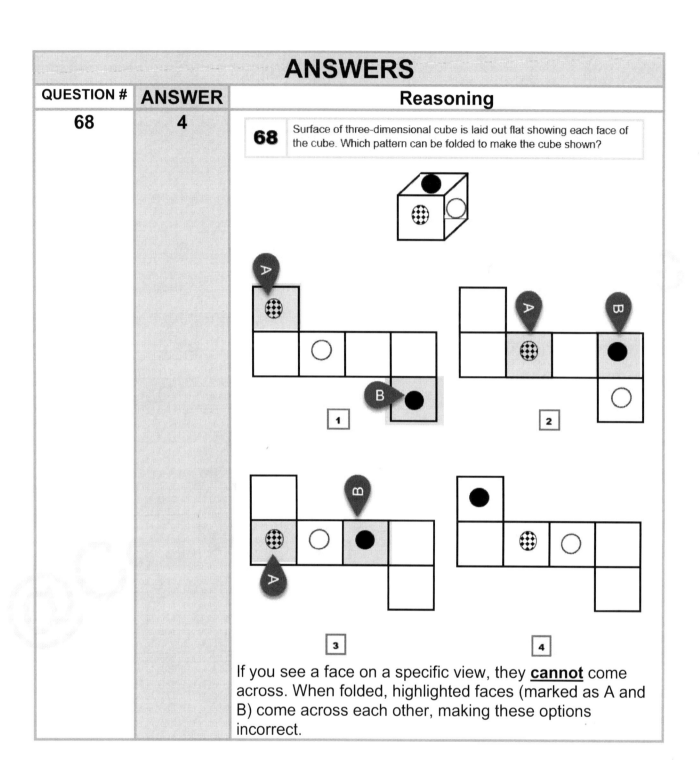 If you see a face on a specific view, they **cannot** come across. When folded, highlighted faces (marked as A and B) come across each other, making these options incorrect.

ANSWERS

QUESTION #	ANSWER	Reasoning
69	1	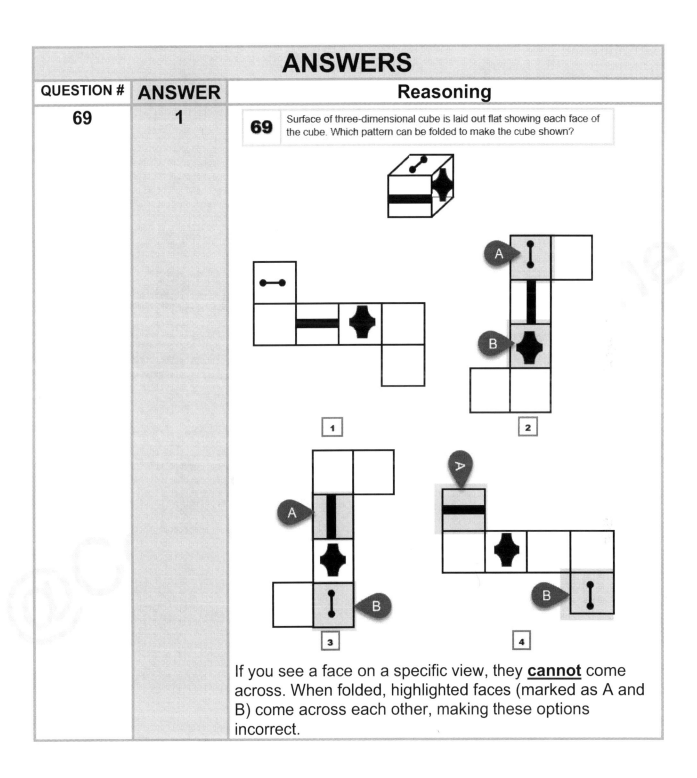 **69** Surface of three-dimensional cube is laid out flat showing each face of the cube. Which pattern can be folded to make the cube shown? If you see a face on a specific view, they **cannot** come across. When folded, highlighted faces (marked as A and B) come across each other, making these options incorrect.

ANSWERS

QUESTION #	ANSWER	Reasoning
70	3	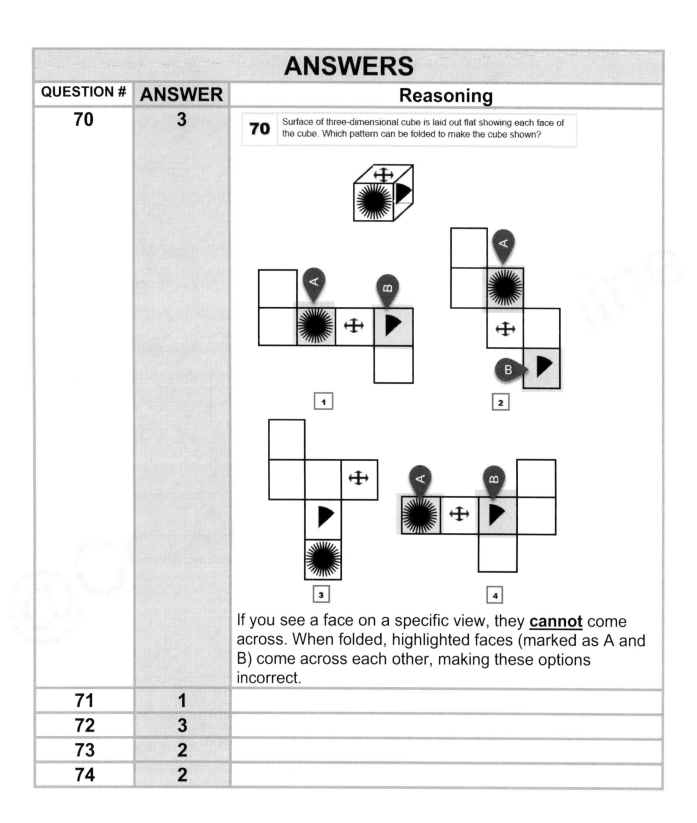 If you see a face on a specific view, they **cannot** come across. When folded, highlighted faces (marked as A and B) come across each other, making these options incorrect.
71	1	
72	3	
73	2	
74	2	

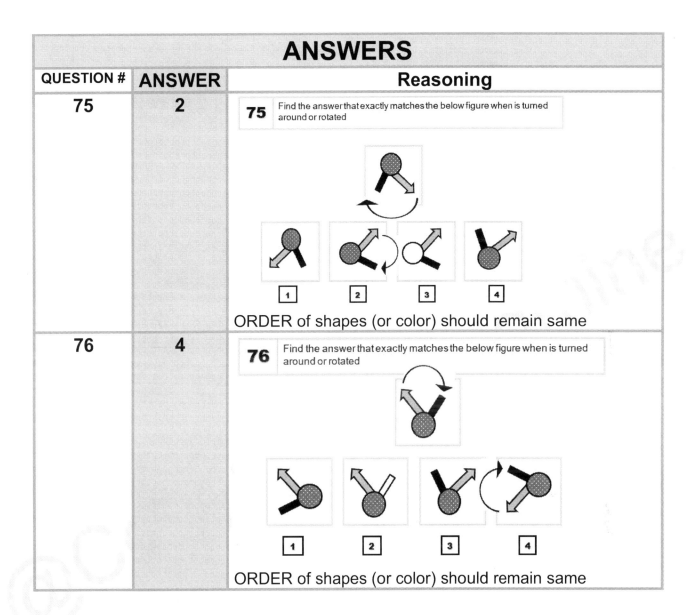

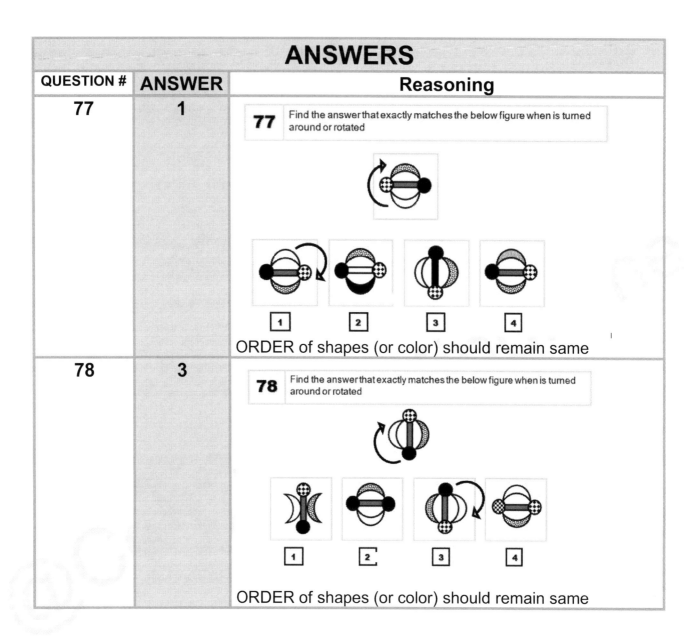

ANSWERS

QUESTION #	ANSWER	Reasoning
79	2	
80	3	

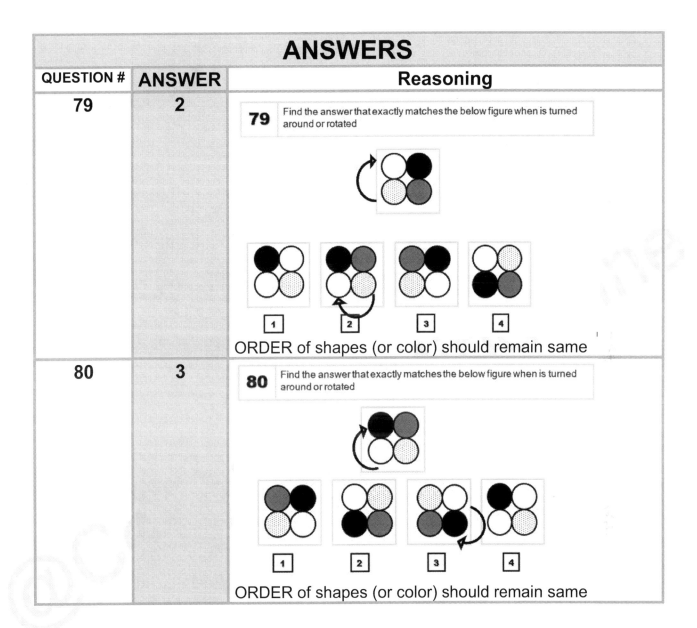

ORDER of shapes (or color) should remain same

ANSWERS

QUESTION #	ANSWER	Reasoning
81	3	81 — Find the answer that exactly matches the below figure when is turned around or rotated. 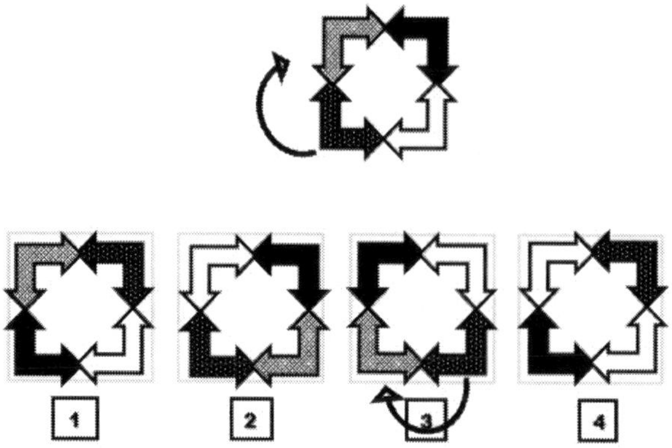 ORDER of shapes (or color) should remain same
82	4	82 — Find the answer that exactly matches the below figure when is turned around or rotated. 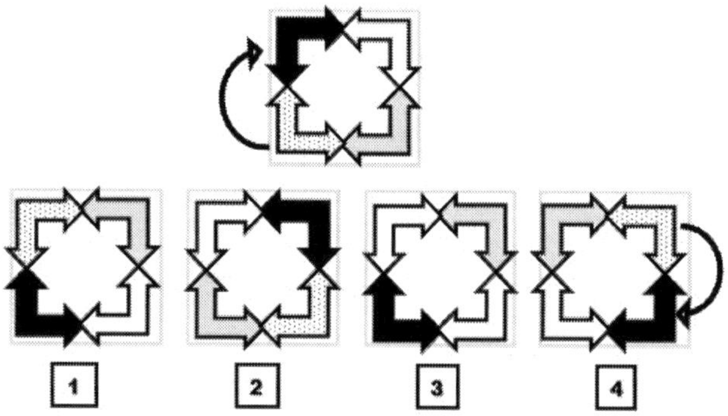 ORDER of shapes (or color) should remain same

ANSWERS

QUESTION #	ANSWER	Reasoning
83	4	
84	2	

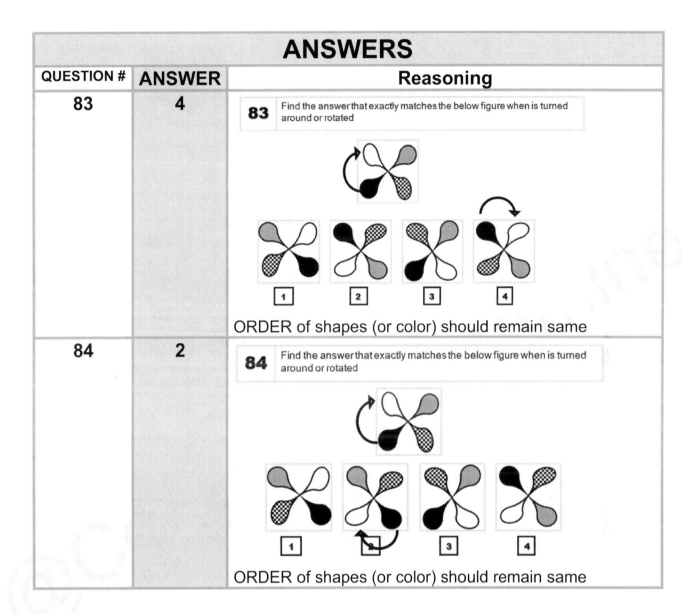

183

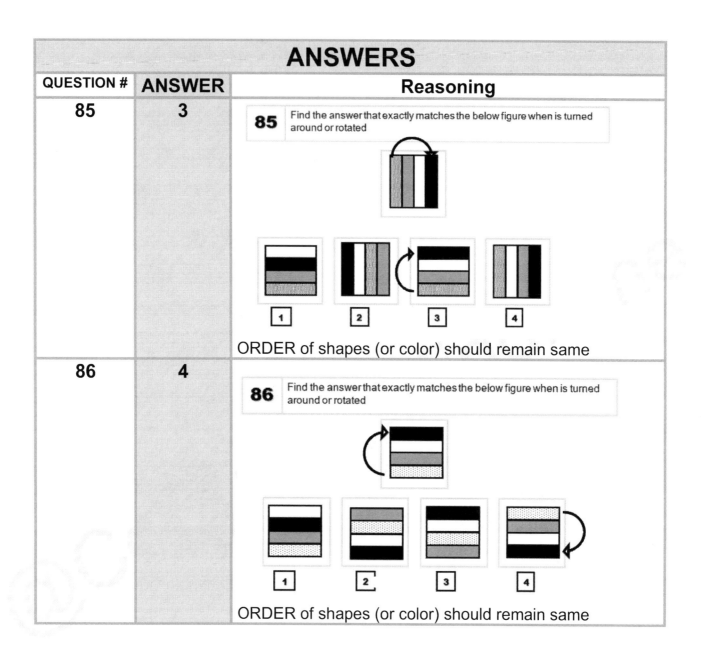

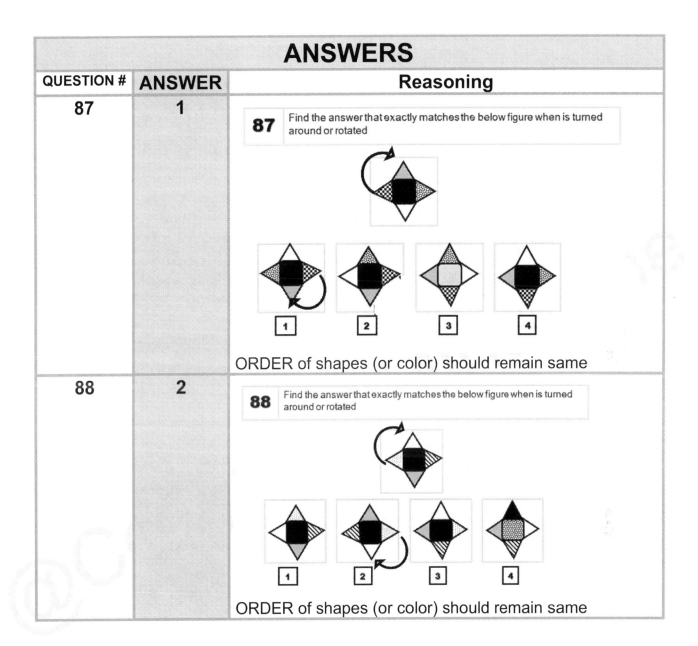

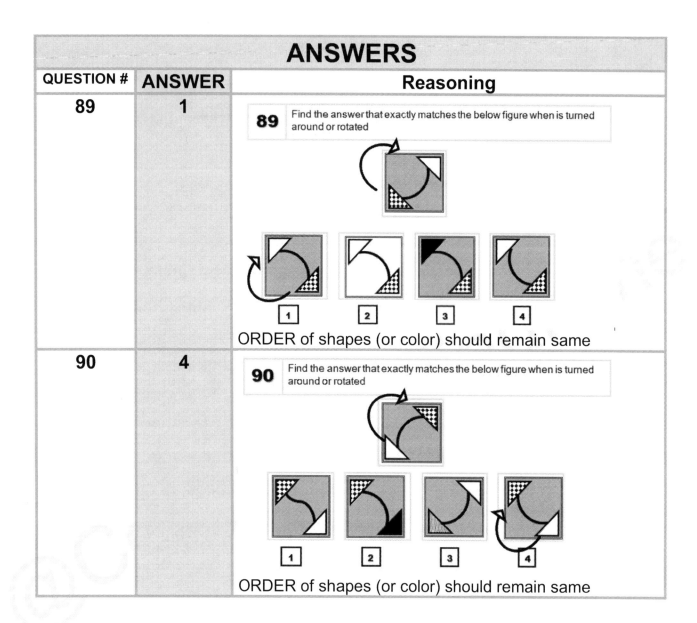

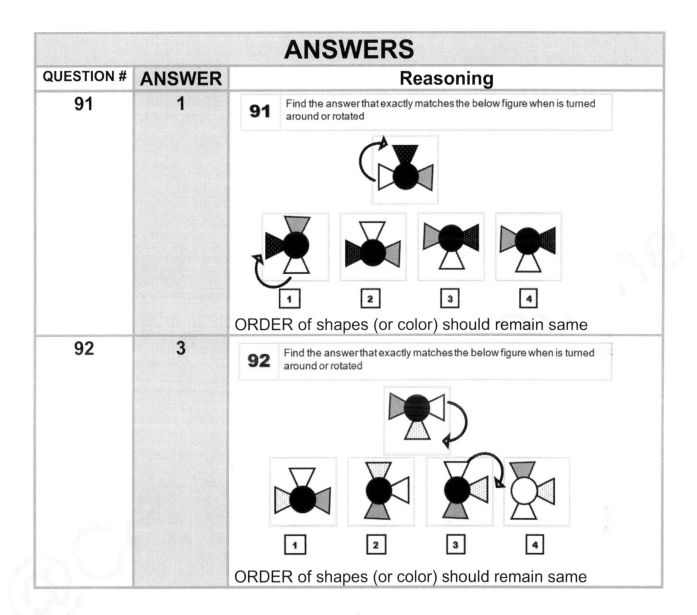

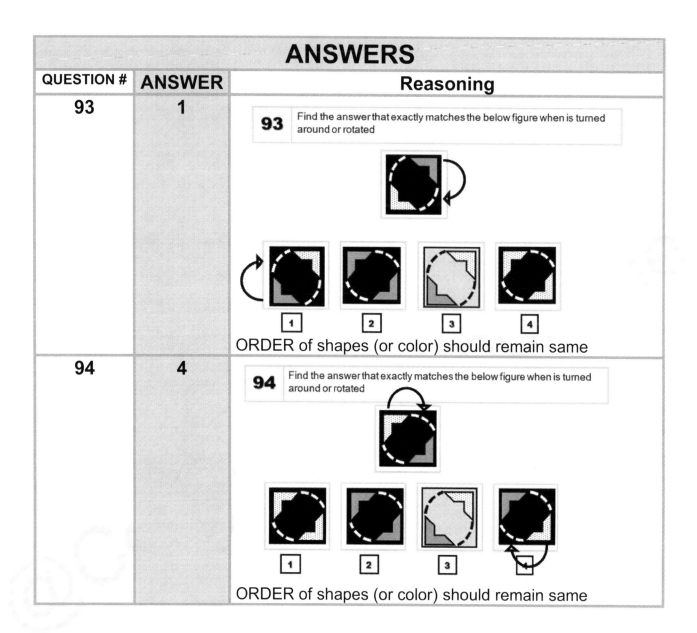

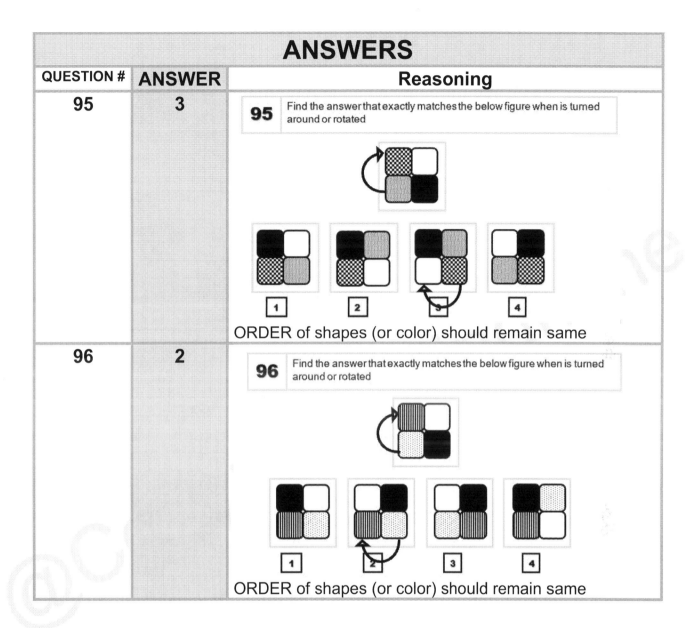

ANSWERS

QUESTION #	ANSWER	Reasoning
97	1	**97** Find the answer that exactly matches the below figure when is turned around or rotated 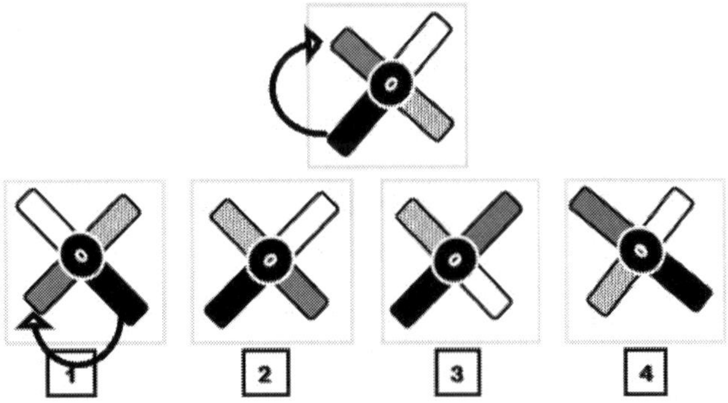 ORDER of shapes (or color) should remain same
98	2	**98** Find the answer that exactly matches the below figure when is turned around or rotated 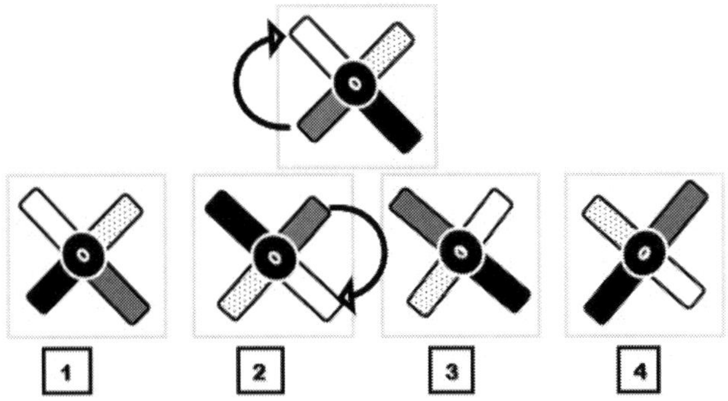 ORDER of shapes (or color) should remain same

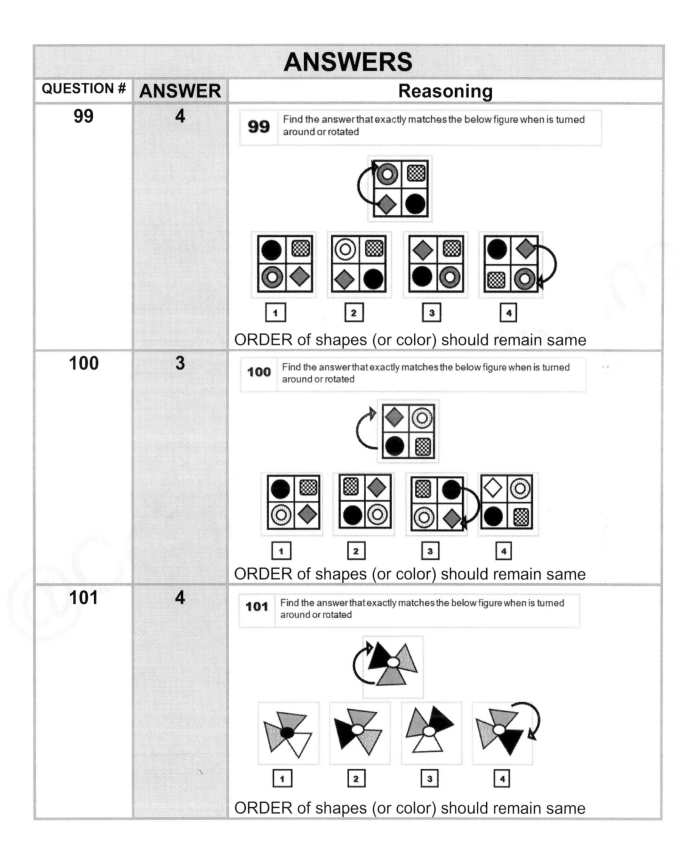

ANSWERS

QUESTION #	ANSWER	Reasoning
102	1	102 Find the answer that exactly matches the below figure when is turned around or rotated 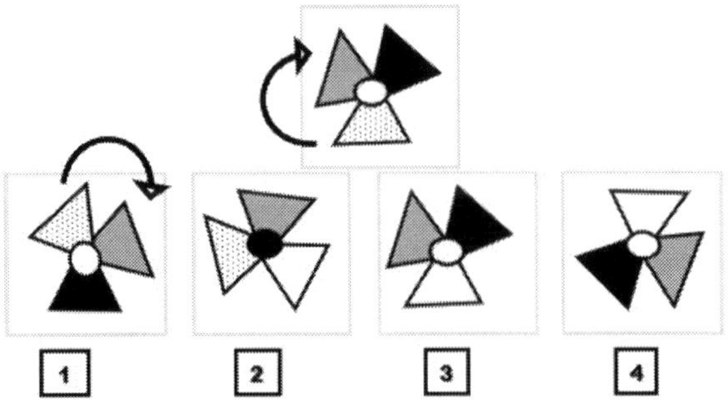 ORDER of shapes (or color) should remain same
103	3	103 Find the answer that exactly matches the below figure when is turned around or rotated 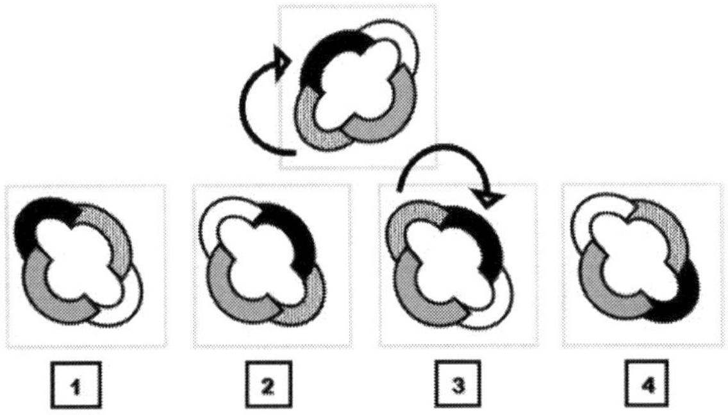 ORDER of shapes (or color) should remain same
104	3	104 Find the answer that exactly matches the below figure when is turned around or rotated 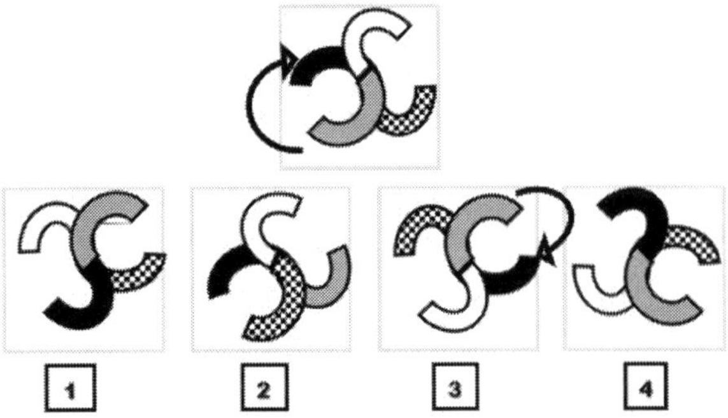

ANSWERS

QUESTION #	ANSWER	Reasoning
		ORDER of shapes (or color) should remain same
105	4	
		ORDER of shapes (or color) should remain same
106	3	Remove a shape in counter clockwise direction
107	4	Add 2 sides; Change pattern to dots
108	4	Change Black shape pattern to dots
109	3	Swap colors
110	5	Cut and remove bottom portion
111	2	Add another half shape
112	3	Swap figures
113	3	Swap colors
114	4	Flip upside down
115	1	Rotate clock wise
116	3	Remove one side
117	5	Figure with half the number of sides
118	1	Rotate clockwise
119	3	Rotate counter clockwise
120	1	Flip upside down
121	5	Rotate counter clockwise
122	4	Swap colors
123	1	Swap colors

ANSWERS

QUESTION #	ANSWER	Reasoning
124	2	Swap colors
125	2	Send the figure to back
126	2	Move half way towards left
127	2	Flip figure sideways and add on the left
128	4	Cut the figure, remove left half
129	2	Flip upside down
130	3	Flip upside down. Add dots to outside box
131	3	Flip upside down
132	5	Flip sideways
133	4	Flip upside down
134	4	Flip upside down
135	2	Flip upside down
136	2	
137	2	
138	3	
139	4	
140	1	

Made in the USA
Middletown, DE
25 October 2024